Finishing Techniques for Crochet

Finishing Techniques for Crochet

Inspiration, projects and techniques for finishing crochet patterns with style

BETTY BARNDEN

SALLY MILNER PUBLISHING

A QUARTO BOOK

Published in 2009 by
Sally Milner Publishing Pty Ltd
734 Woodville Road
BINDA NSW 2583
AUSTRALIA

National Library of Australia Cataloguing-in-Publication entry
Author: Barnden, Betty, 1948-
Title: Finishing techniques for crochet / Betty Barnden.
ISBN: 9781863514132 (pbk.)
Series: Milner craft series
Subjects: Crocheting--Handbooks, manuals, etc.
Dewey Number: 746.434

Conceived, designed and produced by
Quarto Publishing plc
The Old Brewery
6 Blundell Street
London N7 9BH

QUAR: FTC

Senior Editor: Ruth Patrick
Art Editor: Emma Clayton
Designer: Elizabeth Healey
Illustrator: Coral Mula
Copy Editor: Ruth Patrick
Photographer: Phil Wilkins
Proofreader: Sally Maceachern
Indexer: Ann Barrett
Art Director: Caroline Guest

Creative Director: Moira Clinch
Publisher: Paul Carslake

Color separation by Pica Digital Pte Ltd, Singapore
Printed in China by 1010 Printing International Ltd

10 9 8 7 6 5 4 3 2 1

Contents

Ten golden rules for a great finish

Whatever your project, follow these golden rules to help you achieve the great result your time and effort deserve.

1 Collect everything you need

Before you start on any project, make sure you have all the yarn and equipment you will need (see pages 8–9). This sounds simplistic, but if you run out of yarn and the store has sold out, you may never find another matching ball. And if you haven't got a tape measure, or that smaller hook you need for the border, you can start work, but you'll never finish.

2 Check your tension

Always check your tension carefully (see right). Use exactly the same yarn and hook as you intend using for the finished article – the material a hook is made from, and its precise shape, can affect your finished tension. If your tension is not correct, your finished crochet will never be the correct size.

3 Find the rhythm

Don't rush. Sit in a comfortable chair, in a good light. A desk lamp behind the right shoulder gives a good light, if you are right handed. When working with dark-coloured yarns, a white cloth across your lap will help you to see the stitches clearly. If you are right handed, have the ball of yarn to your left, and vice versa. When working stitch patterns, develop the habit of counting in your head, rather like learning to dance: ONE, two, three, ONE, two, three… After the first few rows, a simple stitch pattern will become almost automatic, and your speed will increase.

Measuring tension

1. Make a sample swatch about 15cm (6in) square using your chosen yarn and the recommended hook size (see page 8).

2. Place two pins exactly 10cm (4in) apart along a row of crochet. Count the stitches between the pins.

3. Do the same in the opposite direction to count the rows.

4. If you have too many stitches or rows to 10cm (4in), your work is too tight. Make another swatch with a larger hook and measure the tension again. If you have too few stitches or rows, your work is too loose; try again with a smaller hook.

4 Count, measure and match exactly

Count the base chains and the first couple of rows carefully to make sure you start with the correct number of stitches. Also check the number of stitches in a row from time to time to make sure you haven't made an error.

To count large numbers of base chains or stitches, place a stitch marker every ten or twenty stitches, and when working large pattern repeats, place a stitch marker after every repeat and move it up the work every few rows.

Similarly, when working gradual increasing (for example, every few rows on a sleeve), place a stitch marker on each increased stitch as you make it. Then you can easily count the rows before the next increase.

Check the width and length of your work as the project grows. To measure accurately, lay the crochet on a flat surface. Pat it flat without stretching, and measure the width with a tape measure. Measure the length at the center, not at a side edge.

When working two matching pieces, such as a pair of sleeves, or the fronts of a jacket, count the rows of each section to match the lengths exactly – don't rely on measurements alone.

5 Record your moves

When working from pattern instructions, make a photocopy and use it to check off each pattern repeat, row or section as you complete it. Make notes of any changes such as adjustments to length.

Keep a scrapbook or file of all your projects, with photos if possible. Include copies of patterns with all your notes, along with yarn ball bands, shades (and dyelots) used, hook sizes, etc – this information can be invaluable in the future. You can also note down any difficulties you encounter, whether the yarn was easy to work with or not, and any ideas that occur to you – 'make another in cotton yarn', for example, or 'try a sew-on border next time'.

6 Think ahead

A little forethought can reduce the number of tails that need darning in. This not only saves time, but makes for smoother seams.

Leave long yarn tails where they will be useful later for sewing seams (see page 19).

Don't fasten off a colour if you will need to rejoin it a couple of rows later.

Where an edge will be finished with a grown-on border, leave any yarn tails hanging, then enclose them within the first row of the border (see page 113).

7 Keep your work tidy

When laying your crochet aside, slip the working loop off the hook and onto a stitch marker or safety pin. If you leave it on the hook, the hook may slip out and stitches will unravel. Make a note of your place in the instructions.

To keep your work in progress clean, store it in a fabric bag – plastic bags can cause a build-up of humidity.

8 Be your own critic

From time to time, take a good look at what you've done so far, both close-up and from a distance. Is the pattern consistent? Are those side edges straight?

If you find you've made a mistake, don't think it won't be noticed, because you will always notice it yourself. Slip a stitch marker or a safety pin onto the last correct stitch and unravel the work down to the marker.

9 Assemble carefully

Mismatched, lumpy seams or uneven borders can spoil all your hard work. Pinning and tacking before sewing seams can be very helpful (see pages 22–23). Try out different methods for seams (see pages 19–20), to decide what works best for you and your project.

Don't darn in the yarn tails from the seams until you're happy that all the seams are as neat and even as they can be. Take your time to achieve the result you want.

10 End with a flourish

Add a final touch to make your project unique, by sewing on a decorative pocket (see page 33), adding a flower (see pages 82–83), or embellishing with a fringe or tassels (see pages 80–81). Even a simple touch, such as choosing unusual buttons, can turn a plain garment into something special that will be enjoyed and admired. Be proud of your achievement!

Equipment and materials

The tools required for working crochet are really very simple, and quite inexpensive.

Hooks

These are available in a wide range of sizes, styles and materials.

Hook sizes

Always check your own tension with the exact hook and yarn you intend to use for your project.

There are two systems in general use for sizing crochet hooks. The American system uses numbers for steel hooks, and letters for aluminium and plastic hooks. The International metric system is based on the diameter of the hook shaft measured in millimetres. There is no exact correlation between the two systems, but the table (right) may be used as a guide.

Hook styles

The handles of some crochet hooks have a flattened thumb rest, while others (usually small sizes) have wider plastic handles for a better grip. The tips of some hooks are more pointed than others, and this may affect the actual size of the stitch produced; for yarns that are easily split, a blunter point is preferable.

Hook materials

Steel is mainly used for the smallest sizes, while larger size hooks may be made from aluminium, plastic, wood, resin or bamboo. As a rule, wood and bamboo hooks can help to control very smooth, even slippery yarns, while aluminium hooks slide smoothly through hairy, woolly yarns. Plastic hooks are the lightest in weight.

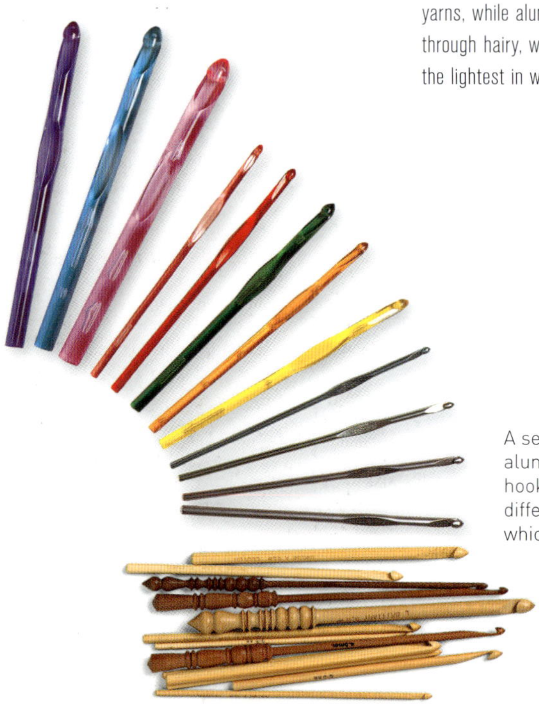

A selection of resin, aluminium and bamboo hooks. Try out hooks in different materials to see which you prefer.

COMPARATIVE CROCHET HOOK SIZES (FROM SMALL TO LARGE)

U.S. steel hooks	U.S. plastic or aluminium hooks	Metric sizes	Suitable for these yarns
14		.6mm	very fine crochet threads
13		.75mm	
12		1mm	
11			
10		1.25mm	
9			
8		1.5mm	
7			
6		1.75mm	2-ply, light fingering
5			
4			
3		2mm	3-ply, fingering
2	B	2.25mm	
1		2.5mm	
0			
00	C	2.75mm	4-ply, fingering, sock
	D	3mm	
	E	3.5mm	sport, double knitting, light worsted
	F		
	G	4mm	
		4.5mm	worsted, aran
	H	5mm	
	I	5.5mm	
	J	6mm	chunky, bulky
	K	6.5mm	
		7mm	
	L	8mm	super chunky, super bulky
	M	9mm	
	N	10mm	

Accessories

In addition to hooks and yarns, the following equipment will also be useful.

Tape measure and ruler

Replace your tape measure from time to time, as the first few inches (or centimetres) can stretch with use. A small ruler is useful for measuring tension (see page 6).

Stitch markers

Stitch markers can be slipped onto your crochet as you work to mark a particular stitch or row, as an aid to counting or working pattern repeats.

Yarn needles

Yarn needles are sometimes called tapestry needles. They have a large eye to take the yarn easily, and a blunt tip, which helps to avoid splitting the yarn as you stitch. They come in a range of sizes and are used for darning in tails, and for sewing seams.

Sharp needles

Needles with sharp points are useful when working embroidery by the method shown on pages 58–59. A large eye is required to easily take the yarn or thread. Ordinary darning needles may be used, or choose specialist embroidery needles, called chenille needles, which are shorter.

Pins

Choose pins with large heads, so they will not slip between the crochet stitches. Glass-headed pins are the best type for blocking (see page 25). Pins with plastic heads are useful when assembling pieces, or use safety pins instead.

Scissors

A pair of small, sharp scissors is essential for cutting yarn cleanly. Never break yarn with your fingers.

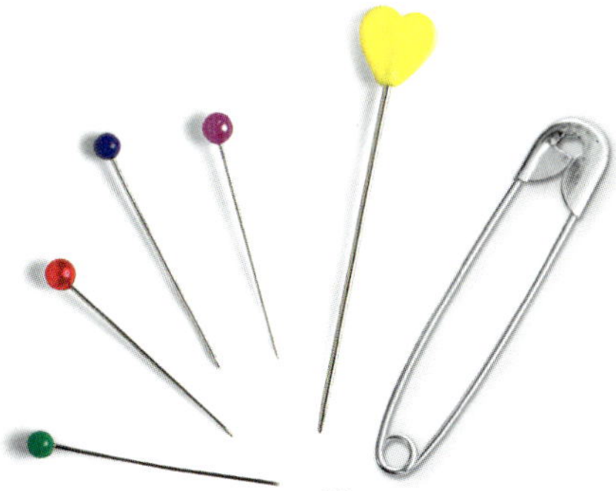

Pins

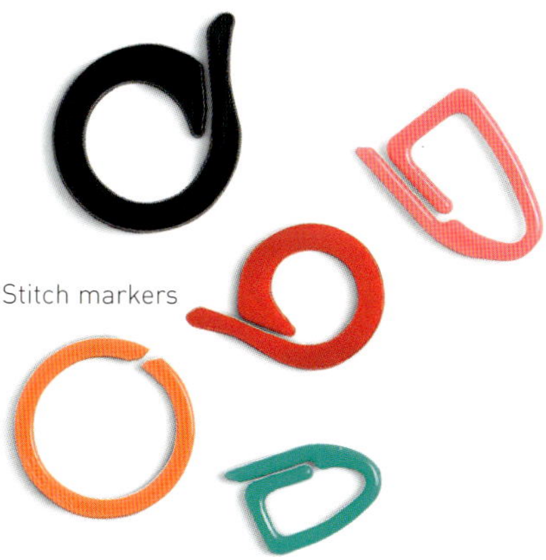

Stitch markers

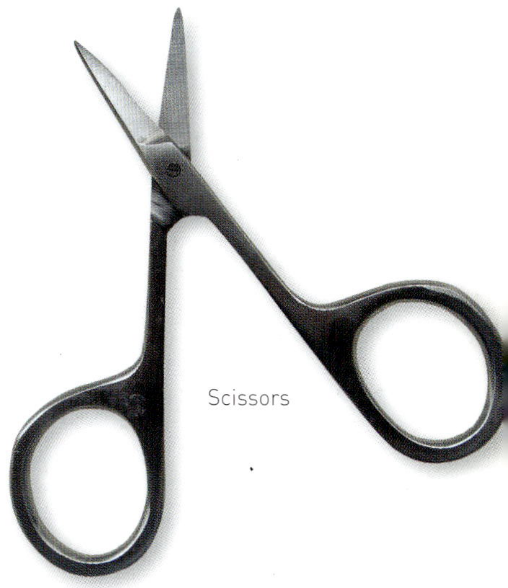

Scissors

Small ruler

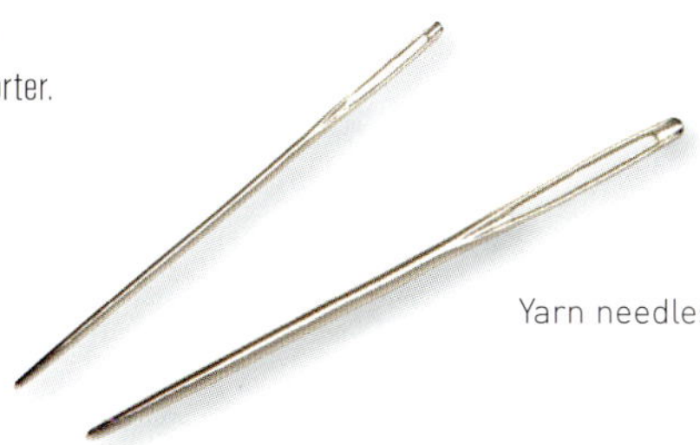

Yarn needles

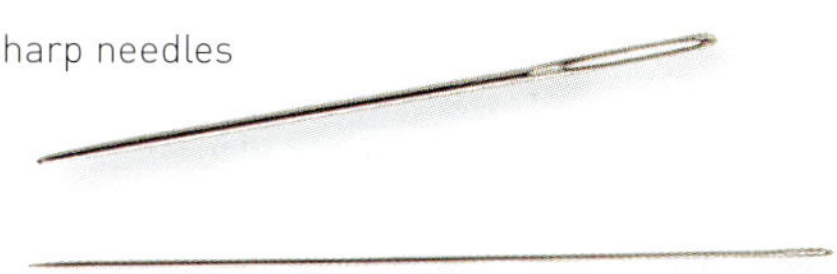

Sharp needles

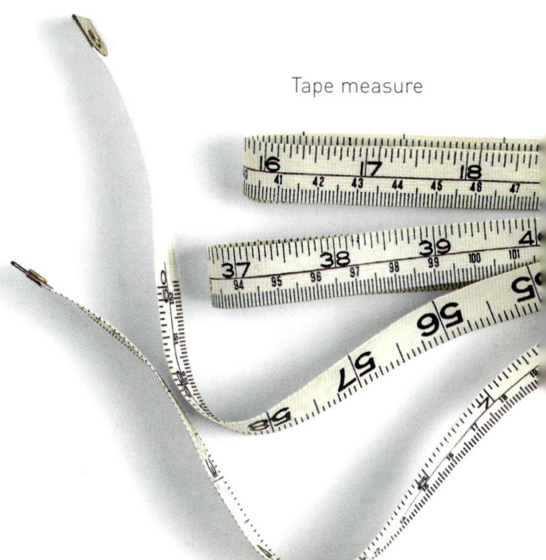

Tape measure

Yarns

There is a huge variety of yarns available today from yarn stores and websites. Specialist crochet yarns are usually fine, smooth cottons, linens or similar fibres, used for traditional fine crochet work. Most knitting yarns are also suitable for crochet, with one or two exceptions, as described in the box, opposite.

Descriptions of yarn weights and types differ from one manufacturer to another, and from one country to another, but below is a rough guide to help you find what you want.

Yarn weights

There are many different weights, or thicknesses, of yarn on the market, and the terminology can be confusing – one manufacturer's aran weight, for example, may be finer or heavier than another's. The examples shown are plain wool and cotton yarns, shown at actual size, to help you understand the different terms used. See page 8 for suitable hook sizes.

Bear in mind that, in general, a crochet fabric in a plain stitch is heavier than a knitted fabric in the same yarn. So a sweater crocheted in, say, aran yarn will be warmer and bulkier (and may require more yarn) than a sweater knitted in the same yarn.

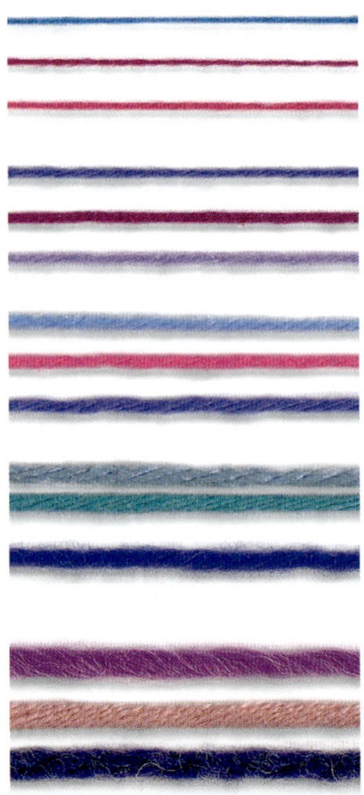

Fine yarn described as crochet thread, two-ply, three-ply or lace-weight is used to make delicate articles, and for fine, lacy crochet using small size hooks.

Four-ply, fingering or sock weight is fine-to-medium weight yarn, often used for baby garments and other small projects.

Double knitting and sport are medium-weight yarns with a wide range of uses. These popular weights are available in a huge choice of colours and fibres.

Aran-weight and worsted yarns are somewhat heavier than sport and double knitting, suitable for many garments and accessories, and again available in a wide range of colours and fibres.

Chunky and bulky yarns are great for quick projects made with a large hook. This category has more variation than any other – some extra-thick yarns are described as extra-bulky, or super-chunky. These yarns will produce very heavy crochet fabric unless an open stitch pattern is used.

Ball band information

The label or band on a ball of yarn can help you decide whether any particular yarn is suitable for your project.

Washing instructions

It is a good idea to keep a ball band from every project as a reference for future washing.

Yarn name and description

Along with the name of the yarn (e.g. Cotton Fine), you will often find a helpful description (e.g. All-season luxury cotton).

Fibre content, weight and yardage

The yardage is a useful indication of the relative weight of a yarn. For example, two double-knitting yarns from different manufacturers may have quite different yardages, indicating that one ball is shorter, and therefore that the yarn is somewhat heavier.

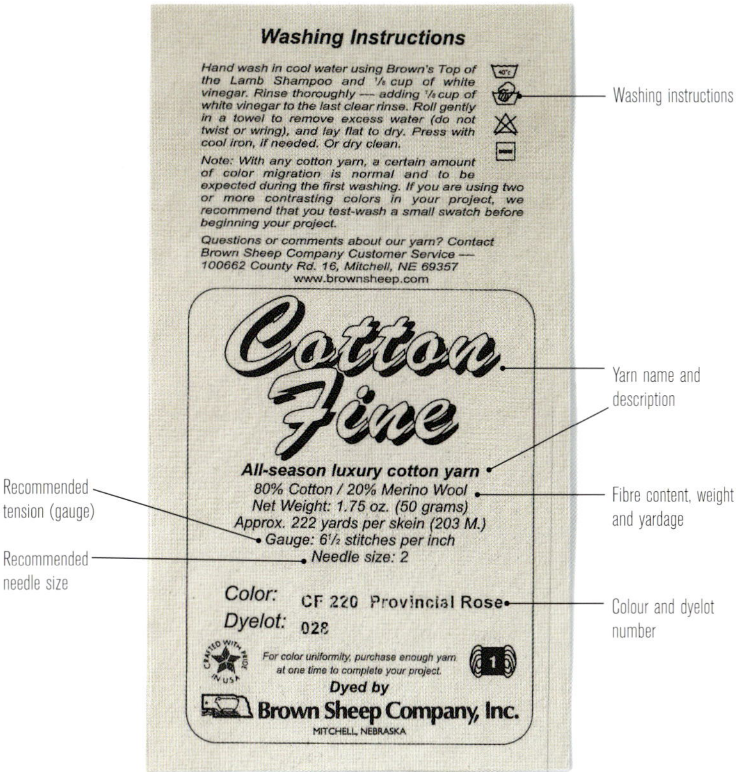

Recommended tension

This is the tension recommended for knitting, and does not apply to crochet.

Recommended needle size

Again, this does not apply to crochet. However, if a recommended knitting needle size is given in International metric sizing (millimetres), a crochet hook of the same metric size will probably be suitable (see page 8).

Colour and dyelot number

When buying more than one ball of the same colour, make sure the dyelot numbers match, otherwise any slight difference in colour may spoil your project.

FANCY YARNS

The decorative knitting yarns available today are very attractive, but some may be difficult to crochet. If you are tempted, buy a single ball to see if the yarn is suitable for crochet, before committing yourself.

Heavily textured yarns can hide the construction of crochet stitches, making it difficult to see where the hook should be inserted. One solution is to choose an open stitch, such as Offset Mesh (see page 89), where the hook is inserted into chain spaces.

Yarn fibres

Yarns may be manufactured from any of the following fibre types, either as single-fibre yarns, or in blends of two or three fibres.

Wool and other animal fibres

Wool from sheep, mohair from goats, angora from rabbits, alpaca, camelhair and other animal fibres may be spun into yarn that is usually warm and soft.

Cotton and other vegetable fibres

Cotton, linen (from flax), hemp, ramie, soya and bamboo are just some of the plants used today to make yarns. In general these yarns are cool and smooth to the touch, with less elasticity than wool.

Silk

Silk threads are obtained from the cocoon of the silkworm, and are found in different qualities from smooth and fine through to coarse and uneven. Pure silk yarn is expensive, so silk is often blended with other fibres (such as cotton).

Synthetic yarns

These are man-made, being derived from coal or petroleum products and spun to resemble natural fibres. They are relatively cheap, hard wearing and often machine washable. They are often blended with natural fibres.

Viscose rayon

This fibre is man-made, but being derived from cellulose (timber) it is not strictly a 'synthetic' product. Viscose rayon fibre is smooth and glossy, and is often blended with matt fibres such as wool or cotton to make fancy yarns.

Part 1:

Construction techniques

Neat edges, accurate shaping and the right method for assembly will all improve the finished appearance of your work. In addition, this chapter contains useful tips on checking and adjusting the fit of a garment, and also how to block or press your work for a perfect finish.

Making neat edges

Improve the final appearance of your crochet by paying attention to the finer details when working lower edges and side edges.

Lower edges

The basic technique of making and counting a base chain (sometimes called a foundation chain, or starting chain) is described on page 108, but here are a few tips to help you begin any project as neatly as possible – remember, a good start is essential to a good finish.

Working into a base chain

After making the number of chains required, straighten them out so they are not twisted. On the first row the hook may be inserted in three different ways:

Under one thread
The easiest method is to insert the hook under the top thread of each chain. However, this makes a rather loose edge, which is fine if you will later be adding an edging, or sewing the edge into a seam.

Under two threads
Insert the hook under the two top threads of each chain to make a firmer edge that is less likely to stretch.

Through back loop
By turning the chain toward you, the back loops become visible. Work the first row into these back loops to make a lower edge that requires no further edging, and closely resembles the top edge of a piece of crochet.

Working extra chains

Sometimes (especially when working a long base chain for a complex stitch pattern) it is a good idea to work several extra chains, just in case you have counted wrongly.

Work the first row with the required number of pattern repeats (or stitches). The slipknot and extra chains can be quickly unpicked with a yarn needle before assembling the project.

Side edges

A row of crochet stitches normally begins with one, two or more turning chains, which make the first stitch of the row. On the next row, the last stitch is worked into the top of these chains.

1 When you reach the end of a row, turn the work in the direction shown.

2 At the end of the next row, the turning chains will then be seen as shown here. This makes it easy to insert the hook under two threads of the top chain, to work the last stitch of the row.

When a row begins with chains that are then immediately worked into, it is neater to turn the work in the other direction. For example, when working step increasing (see page 15), the step begins with several chains. If you turn the work from right to left, then work the chains, they will present themselves like a base chain.

Basic shaping

Projects can involve shaping, by increasing and/or decreasing the total number of stitches. Shaping as neatly as possible will help you obtain a good finish.

Increasing

When working a plain stitch, such as rows of double crochet, treble crochet (shown here) or double trebles, an increase is made simply by working two (or more) times into the same stitch. Such an increase may be worked at the beginning or end of a row, or anywhere in between.

Basic increase

Two (or more) stitches may be worked in the same place, anywhere along a row. To increase several stitches evenly across a row, space such increases at equal intervals.

Beginning of a row

At the start of a row, work the usual number of turning chain (three shown here). Do not skip the first stitch, as you normally would, but work a stitch into it. One stitch has now been increased.

End of a row

To increase one stitch at the end of a row, work two stitches into the top of the turning chain of the previous row.

Decreasing

A basic decrease is made by working two (or more) stitches together.

Basic decrease

This example shows two trebles worked together, but the same principle applies to other stitches: work the first stitch up to the last 'yarn round hook, pull through' (leaving two loops on the hook), then work the next stitch in the same way (making three loops on the hook), yarn round hook, and pull through all the loops on the hook. The two stitches are joined together at the top, and treated as a single stitch on the next row.

Beginning of a row

At the beginning of a row, work one turning chain less than the usual number (for example, 2 ch instead of 3 ch when working in treble crochet). Skip the first stitch in the usual way and work one stitch into the next stitch. Work the last stitch of the next row into the first stitch; do not work into the turning chain.

End of a row

Work the last two stitches together as above. If the previous row is unshaped, the last hook insertion will be made into the top of the turning chain. If the previous row began with a decrease, the last insertion will be made into the first stitch of the previous row, not into the turning chain.

Step shaping

Sometimes you need to increase or decrease several stitches at the beginning and/or end of a row, forming a step (or a series of steps).

Step decreasing at the beginning of a row

Slip stitch is used to form this step. Work one slip stitch in the top of each stitch to be decreased, and one slip stitch into the next stitch. Work the usual number of turning chains, skip the stitch at the base of the chain, and continue along the row as required.

Step decreasing at the end of a row

The step decrease is worked as follows: simply leave the required number of stitches (including the turning chain) unworked, turn and begin the next row.

Step increasing at the beginning of a row

Work one chain for each extra stitch required, plus the usual number of turning chains minus one – for the six extra trebles shown here, (6 + 2) = 8 chains. Beginning in the appropriate chain counted from the hook (fourth chain shown here), work the extra stitches, then continue along the row. (The turning chain at the beginning of the row counts as the first extra stitch).

Step increasing at the end of a row

Extended stitches may be used to add any number of stitches at the end of a row. See also page 117.

Wrap the yarn round the hook as many times as is required for the stitch in use (e.g. one wrap for treble crochet), insert the hook in the same place as the last stitch, yarn round hook, and pull through a loop. Then make the extension: yarn round hook, pull through the first loop on the hook. Complete the stitch in the usual way. For the next stitch, wrap the yarn round the hook as required, insert the hook in the base of the previous stitch and work the extended stitch as before.

INCREASING FOR SMOOTH SIDE EDGES

Where the side edges will be sewn into a seam, it is useful to work the shaping one stitch in from the sides, to make the edges straighter.

- At the beginning of a row (shown at right), work the turning chain, skip the first stitch, then work two stitches into the next stitch.
- At the end of a row, work two stitches into the last stitch and one stitch into the turning chain.

Advanced shaping

Keeping a fancy stitch pattern constant while working shaping can be tricky. The stitches and method used will depend on the particular pattern. Crochet instructions normally give the method in detail, but it helps if you understand the principles involved.

Shaping in a background stitch

Some stitch patterns are based on a background stitch, such as the bobble stitch pattern below. This is based on rows of treble and double crochet, with bobbles placed in a regular arrangement.

Bobble stitch

This is the basic pattern used for the examples on this page, without any shaping:

Requires a multiple of 6 sts, plus 1. Base chain (x 6) + 3.

Row 1: 1 tr in 4th ch from hook, * 1 ch, skip 1 ch, 4 dtr tog in next ch, 1 ch, skip 1 ch, 1 tr in each of next 3 ch *, repeat from * to * ending 1 tr in each of last 2 ch.

Row 2: 1 ch, skip first tr, 1 dc in next tr, * 1 dc in ch-sp, 1 ch, skip top of group, 1 dc in ch-sp, 1 dc in each of 3 tr *, repeat from * to * ending 1 dc in last tr, 1 dc in 3rd of 3 ch.

Row 3: 3 ch, skip first dc, 1 tr in next dc, * 1 ch, skip 1 dc, 4 dtr tog in ch-sp, 1 ch, skip 1 dc, 1 tr in each of next 3 dc, * repeat from * to * ending 1 tr in last dc, 1 tr in 1 ch.

Repeat rows 2 and 3 as required.

KEY

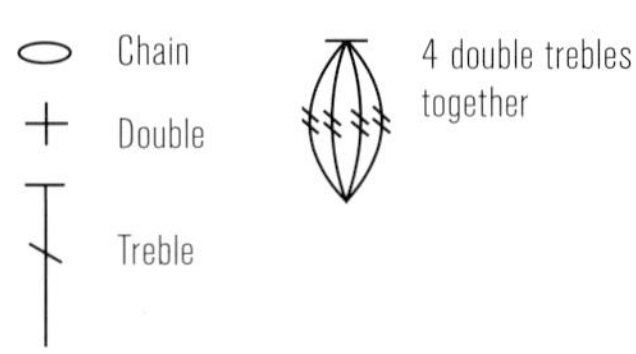

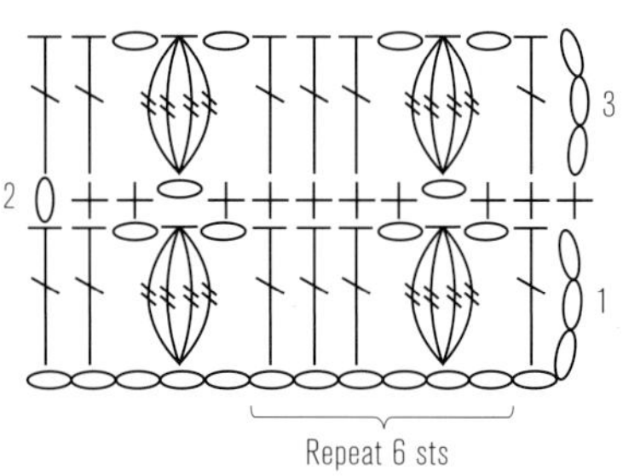

Increasing in pattern

Increases are made at each edge in the background stitch, until there are enough extra stitches at each side for another repeat of the pattern.

The chart shows how one stitch is increased at the beginning and end of alternate rows, keeping the pattern constant.

On inc row 9, sufficient extra stitches have been made for an extra group of 4 dtr tog at each side. On inc row 12, the total number of stitches is again a multiple of 6, plus 1. To continue increasing, repeat inc rows 1–12, or continue in the basic pattern without further shaping.

KEY

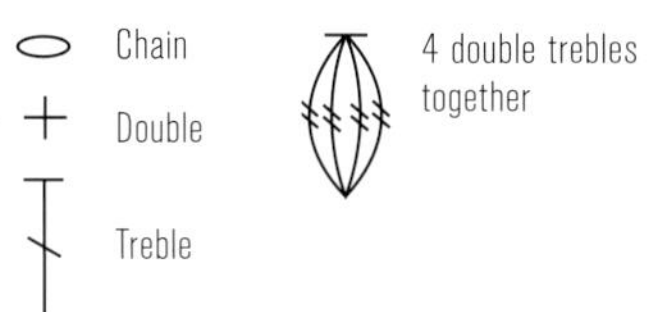

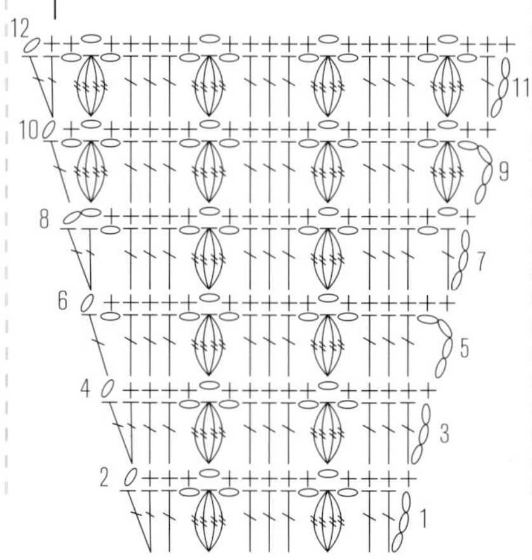

Decreasing in pattern

Decreases are shown here at each end of every right-side row. The chart shows how one stitch is decreased at the beginning and end of alternate rows, keeping the pattern constant.

On dec row 5 there are no longer sufficient stitches to work a bobble stitch group. On dec row 12, the total number of stitches is again a multiple of 6, plus 1. To continue decreasing, repeat dec rows 1–12; or continue in the basic pattern without further shaping.

KEY

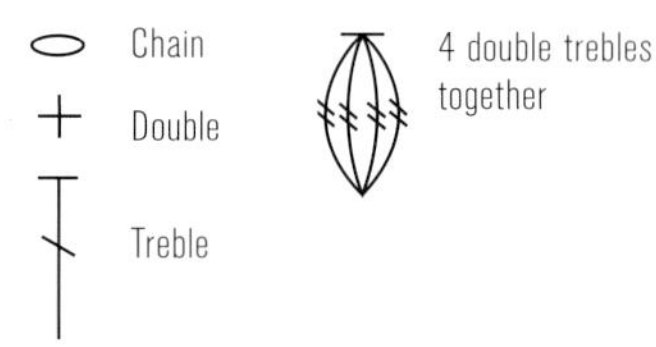

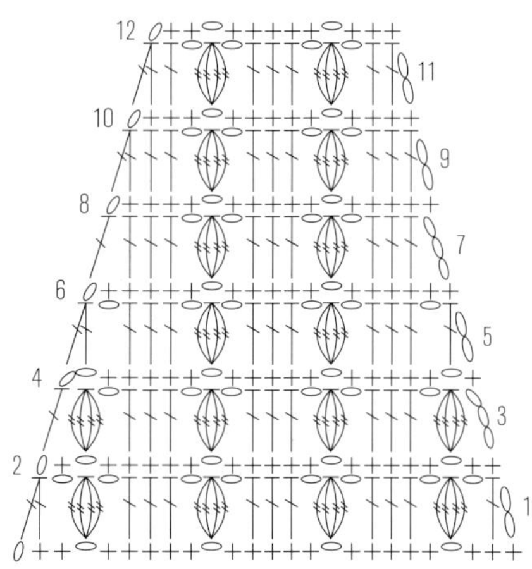

Shaping more complex patterns

Other stitch patterns require different approaches, and it is not possible to illustrate all the variations. If you are puzzled by the shaping given in pattern instructions, work a small sample piece so that you understand what the pattern designer intends, before spending time shaping a large piece.

This Star stitch pattern is based on groups of trebles, and lends itself to increasing or decreasing one whole group at a time, which dictates the angles of the resulting sloping edges.

Basic star stitch

This is the basic pattern used for the examples on this page, without any shaping:

Requires a multiple of 4 stitches, plus 2. Base chain: (x 4) + 5.

Row 1: [1 tr, 1 ch] 3 times in 6th ch from hook, 1 tr in same ch, * skip 3 ch, [1 tr, 1 ch] 3 times in next ch, 1 tr in same ch, * repeat from * to * ending skip 2 ch, 1 tr in last ch.

Row 2: 3 ch, skip [2 tr, 1 ch, 1 tr], * [1 tr, 1 ch] 3 times in next ch sp (the centre ch-sp of group), 1 tr in same ch-sp, skip [1 tr, 1 ch, 2 tr, 1 ch, 1 tr], * repeat from * to * ending in centre of last group, skip [1 tr, 1 ch, 1 tr], 1 tr in top of turning ch.

Repeat row 2 as required.

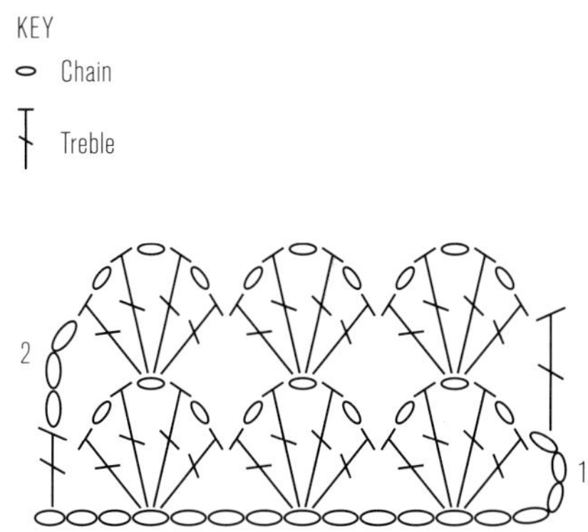

Increasing in pattern

One whole pattern repeat is increased at each edge, at each end of every row:

At the beginning of inc row 1, work 7 ch. The first three of these ch are equivalent to half the top edge of a group; the remaining 4 ch stand for the 1 tr, 1 ch at the beginning of the extra group. Then work the remaining sts of the extra group into the fifth ch from the hook. At the end of the row, an extra-long treble is worked into the turning chain of the previous row, then the remaining stitches of the extra group are worked into the stem of the long treble.

On following increase rows (inc row 2), the long treble at the end is worked into the sixth of 7 ch at the beginning of the previous row, to keep the pattern constant. To work further increases, repeat inc row 2.

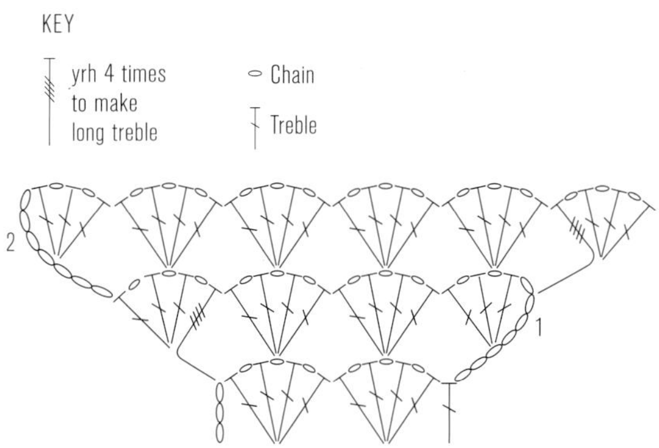

Decreasing in pattern

One whole pattern repeat is decreased here at each end of every row, keeping the pattern constant.

At the beginning of dec row 1, work 1 ss into each stitch to the centre of the first group, then 2 ch (1 ch less than the usual number of turning ch for a treble crochet, as when decreasing at the beginning of a row). Work the first group into the second group of the previous row. At the end of the row, the last group is worked into the next to last group of the previous row. This last group ends with 2 tr tog, inserting the hook into [same place as previous tr, and centre of last group].

Dec row 2 is worked in the same way, but with fewer slip stitches at the beginning. To decrease further, repeat dec row 2.

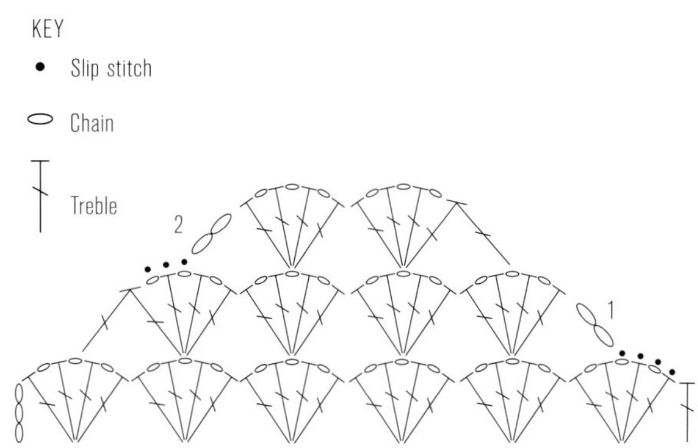

Assembling your project

Whatever your project, neat and accurate assembly is key to achieving a good finish. First, secure any yarn tails so they will not work loose, then sew or crochet the seams. Try out different seaming methods using contrasting yarn – then you will see which method gives the neatest result, and the contrasting yarn may be easily unpicked.

Tidying yarn tails

Before beginning to work the seams, deal with any unwanted yarn tails. When working any piece of crochet, think ahead to the assembly process: long yarn tails may be left at the beginning and end of a piece, or anywhere along an edge to be seamed, and used later for sewing seams. Unwanted tails may be enclosed as you work (see page 113), or darned in as follows using a blunt-tipped yarn needle (see page 9).

Darning in at the lower edge

At the lower edge of the piece, thread the starting tail into a yarn needle. With the wrong side of work facing, pass the needle through the bases of the stitches of the first row for at least 5cm (2in). Pull through and snip off the excess.

Darning in at the upper edge

At the upper edge of a piece, the tail should be woven through the backs of the tops of the stitches, on the wrong side of the work, for 5cm (2in). Pull through and trim the excess.

Darning in at the side edge

Tails on a side edge may be passed through the bases of the stitches along any row for about 5cm (2in).

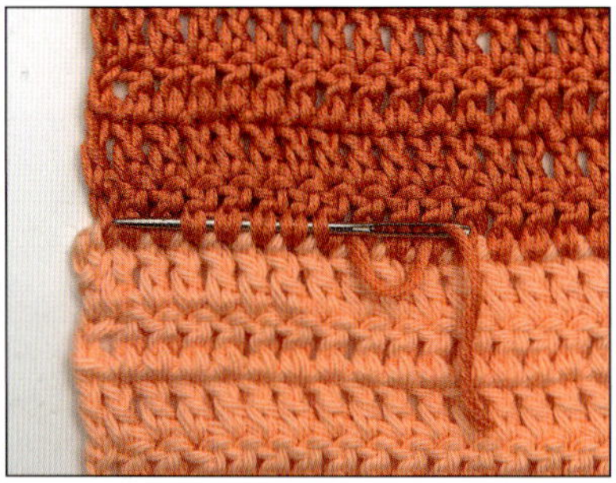

Darning in slippery yarns

Slippery yarns may need to be secured more firmly. Leave a tail of at least 15cm (6in). With the wrong side of the work facing, darn the tail in as at left, then take the needle over a single thread of the next stitch of the row, and back again in the opposite direction for at least 2.5cm (1in). Pull through and snip off short.

Darning in for openwork patterns

With the wrong side facing, thread the tail into a yarn needle and run it through the backs of the stitches for about 5cm (2in), as before. Change direction to suit the pattern, so the tail will not show when viewed from the right side.

Sewing seams

As a rule, it is best to use the same yarn as the project for sewing seams. However, if the yarn is bulky or frays easily, you can use a finer yarn of similar colour and fibre content. For multi-colour pieces, choose a colour that blends in as much as possible, or make a feature of a crochet seam (see page 20) in a contrasting colour.

If your crochet pieces do not lie flat, or look uneven, block or press them (see pages 24–25) before sewing together. Otherwise, block the completed article after assembly.

Always use a blunt-tipped yarn needle (see page 9) and use safety pins to hold pieces together while you stitch.

Backstitch seam

Backstitch makes a firm seam when joining the side edges of crochet pieces, and gives a neat finish around curved seams such as armholes. However, it can be bulky, so it is not always suitable for children's garments.

Pin the two edges with right sides together, matching the row ends carefully. (Where row ends do not match, such as an armhole seam, spread any fullness evenly). Thread a yarn needle with matching yarn and secure at the right, leaving a 10cm (4in) tail. Work a line of backstitch from right to left as shown, close to the edges, either one whole stitch or one half-stitch in from the edges, depending on the stitch pattern. At each end of the seam, darn in the tails (see opposite).

Overcast seam

This seam is the least bulky method for joining side edges, and therefore the most suitable for baby garments. However, it can be difficult to work neatly, and is not particularly strong.

Lay the pieces side by side on a flat surface with wrong sides uppermost. Pin them together with safety pins, matching row ends. Secure the yarn at the lower edge with a backstitch. Pass the needle from right to left under one thread from each edge and pull through. Repeat, matching the row ends exactly. Draw the edges together, but not so tightly that the seam is shorter than the work, or the seam may break in use. Secure at the top with a backstitch and darn in the yarn tails as before.

Flat woven seam

This seam is often used for joining the top (and bottom) edges of crochet pieces, and makes a flat seam with no ridge, suitable for baby garments. It gives a neat finish when joining squares and hexagons (see page 121).

Place the pieces on a flat surface with wrong sides uppermost, and the edges touching. Thread the yarn into a yarn needle and secure at right leaving a 10cm (4in) tail. Link the two edges together by passing the needle up under one thread from each edge, then down under the next thread from each edge. Repeat along the seam, matching the stitches exactly. Draw the edges together quite firmly as you stitch. At the end, secure with a backstitch, then darn in the tails (see opposite).

Ladder stitch seam

This seam can give the neatest finish of all, but it does form a slight ridge on the wrong side. It is worked with the right side facing, so you can see the final appearance as work proceeds.

Lay the pieces side by side on a flat surface, with right sides facing. Pin together with safety pins, matching row ends. Secure the yarn at the lower edge. Work evenly spaced stitches in a loose zigzag from one edge to the other, making each stitch about the length of one crochet chain. Work either one whole stitch in from the each edge, or through the centres of the edge stitches and turning chains, depending on the stitch pattern. Tighten the stitches as work proceeds. Secure the yarn at the top and darn in the yarn tails as before.

Working crochet seams

Any crochet seam forms a ridge, and may be quite bulky. However, crochet seams are strong and flexible, and may be worked on the right side of a garment or other project as a decorative detail. Use a matching, finer yarn to make a crochet seam less bulky. For seams on the right side of the work, try using a contrasting colour for extra interest.

Slip-stitch seam

This seam may be worked to join two side edges, as shown, or two upper/lower edges. It may be worked on the right or wrong side of the work.

For a seam on the wrong side of the work, pin the pieces with right sides together. Working from right to left, hold the yarn behind the work and insert the hook through both layers, either 1 whole stitch in from each edge, or through the centre of the first stitch on each edge. Pull through a loop of yarn. Insert the hook again a little further along the seam, pull through another loop, and pull the new loop through the loop on the hook. Repeat to the end. Cut the yarn and pull it through the last loop, then darn in the tails (see page 18).

On side edges, make the slip stitches a little longer than the length of one crochet chain – when joining the side edges of treble crochet, for example, 2 slip stitches in the side edge of every row usually gives a neat result. On upper/lower edges, work 1 slip stitch through every pair of stitches along the edge.

Double crochet seam

This seam may be worked on two side edges, or two upper/lower edges, as shown. It may also be worked as a feature on the right side of the work. The edges are enclosed within a row of double crochet.

For a seam on the wrong side, pin the pieces with right sides together. Working from right to left, hold the yarn behind the work and insert the hook through both layers, pull through a loop. Work in double crochet through both edges together. At the end, cut the yarn, pull it through the last loop, and darn in the tails (see page 18).

On upper/lower edges, make 1 double crochet for every pair of stitches along the edge. On side edges, try out a short length of seam to find a suitable spacing for the double crochet seam – on pieces made in double crochet, for example, one seam stitch per row is usual. You can also change the hook size to make the seam a little tighter or looser.

Double crochet and chain seam

This seam is less bulky than the double crochet seam at left, and also lies flatter. It is usually worked on the wrong side of the work.

Begin as for the double crochet seam at left, but instead of double crochet, work * 1 double crochet, 1 chain *, repeat from * to *, and space the double crochet stitches further apart. End with a double crochet stitch and fasten off as before.

Joining blocks

When joining crochet blocks for a shawl or blanket, use a method that will be equally neat on both sides. Blocks worked 'in the round' have the tops of stitches all around the outside edges, so they may be neatly joined with the Flat woven seam or the Double crochet seam. The latter may be worked in a single bold colour to visually link multicoloured blocks together.

Joining square blocks

Whichever seam you choose, it is a good idea to lay out all the blocks in the correct order on your work surface (or on the floor). If you then work the seams from the right side, you can pick up each piece in turn and so avoid time-wasting mistakes. If you want to work a seam from the wrong side, you must lay all the blocks out, wrong side up, so that the order will be correct when they are joined together.

1 First work all the seams in one direction, matching the stitches of each edge exactly. Here, a double crochet seam is being worked in a contrasting colour. Pull firmly when passing from one pair of blocks to the next.

2 Then work all the seams in the opposite direction. At the corner junctions, pull the yarn firmly across the top of the previous seam.

Joining blocks with picots

Some lacy blocks (both squares and hexagons) are designed to be joined together as each block is completed, by linking the picots to previous blocks. Working picots is shown on page 116.

1 To join adjacent picots, work to the centre chain of a picot, insert the hook from below into the corresponding picot of the previous block and work 1 slip stitch (which replaces 1 chain). Complete the picot.

2 Subsequent blocks may be joined on one, two or more sides of the last round. At the corners, work the slip stitch joining the picots as before, but inserting the hook into the picot diagonally opposite.

Checking and adjusting fit

If you are making a garment for yourself or a member of the family, you can check the size and fit as the work proceeds, and make minor adjustments if necessary. Here's a step-by-step guide to help you avoid wasting time by having to unravel and rework your project:

Check the instruction measurements

Most commercial patterns include measurements such as actual chest measurement, length of garment to shoulder, sleeve length, etc. Where measurements are quoted in both inches and centimetres, choose which system to follow and stick to it throughout – don't chop and change between the two systems, because the equivalent measurements are not always 100 per cent accurate.

- Measurements should be taken, wearing whatever clothes you would normally wear under the garment you are making. If the person you are making the garment for is not around, try to borrow a similar garment that fits them, and measure that.
- Note that the 'chest measurement' is normally the measurement taken from the body, but the 'actual (garment) measurement' may include several inches of 'ease', depending on the style of the garment.
- Choose the garment size with the most closely corresponding chest measurement. It is often quite easy to adjust the length, but far more difficult to adjust the width of garment pieces.
- Front(s), Back, and Sleeves are normally lengthened or shortened just below the armhole at a point where no shaping is being worked. Make a note of the length(s) you require.
- For children's garments, you may decide to choose the next size up.

Try it for size

Instructions usually begin with the Back of a garment, but if you are in doubt about the fit, try beginning with the Front (or one front of a jacket, as shown), as this will give you a better idea of the fit.

Use safety pins to fix the crochet to a T-shirt or similar garment, matching the shoulders and armholes as nearly as possible, and try it on.

Adjust the body length if necessary by unravelling down to the armhole shaping, then working a few more rows to lengthen, or unravelling a few rows to shorten. Then rework the armhole shaping. Work the Back (and the remaining Front) to match the new length.

For a garment with sleeves, try to avoid changing the depth of the armhole – the sleeve width and shaping will then also require adjusting, which can be tricky (see opposite).

The Back, one Front and one Sleeve of this jacket have been tacked together to test the fit of the sleeve and armhole. For tacked, use a smooth yarn such as double knitting cotton, in a contrasting colour, and a blunt-tipped yarn needle. Try on the tacked pieces, pinning the free shoulder to your clothes.

If the sleeve and armhole fit is too tight, (but the body width is correct), you may need to work the armhole depth to match the next larger size on the instructions, then rework the sleeve from the next larger size.

If a sleeve and armhole fit is too loose, try including shoulder pads as at right before you unravel your work.

Final touches

The fit of the neckline and shoulders is often the key to a successful garment. If the shoulders are too wide, try reinforcing the shoulder seams by working a row of slip stitch firmly from the corner of one shoulder, across the back of the neck to the corner of the other shoulder. You can also reinforce a loose neckline in the same way.

Shoulder pads

Adding shoulder pads can improve the fit of a garment with set-in sleeves. You can purchase ready-made pads, but pads made in matching yarn work well for crochet garments. These instructions apply to double knitting, but are easily adapted to other yarn weights. For yarns heavier than double knitting, a single strand will make a substantial pad.

Using yarn double and a size 5mm hook, work 3 ch.

Row 1: 1 dc in 2nd ch from hook, 2 dc in next ch.

Inc row: 1 ch, 1 dc in first dc, 1 dc in each dc ending 2 dc in 1 ch. (6 sts).

Repeat inc row an even number of times, until piece measures approximately 12.5cm (5in) across top edge.

Next row: 1 ch, 1 dc in first dc, 1 dc in each dc to centre 4 dc, [2dctog] twice, 1 dc in each dc, ending 2 dc in 1 ch.

Following row: as inc row.

Repeat last 2 rows, 2 or 3 more times until piece measures approx. 15–17.5cm (6–7in) across top edge. Fasten off.

Sew the shoulder pad in place to the inside of the garment, matching the centre of the pad to the shoulder seam, with the lower point toward the neck edge, and the top edge of the pad lying along the top of the sleeve. Sew down the three corners only.

Blocking and pressing

Improve the appearance of your finished crochet by blocking or pressing, to even out uneven stitches and 'set' the shape.

- **Use blocking for:** yarns labelled 'do not press' (such as synthetic and textured yarns), boldly textured stitches and projects including several different yarns.
- **Use pressing for:** yarns labelled with a recommended ironing temperature (usually natural fibres, such as wool or cotton).

How to block

You can block a garment after assembly, as shown below, or block the pieces separately if you prefer.

1 Wash the crochet gently by hand in lukewarm water, using a small amount of suitable gentle detergent. Squeeze gently – do not rub. Leave the crochet to soak for a few minutes to make sure the water penetrates all the fibres. Do not lift the crochet out, but support it with your hand as you drain away the water. The aim is to avoid stretching the work. Gently squeeze out the excess water. Do not wring. Rinse in three changes of lukewarm water.

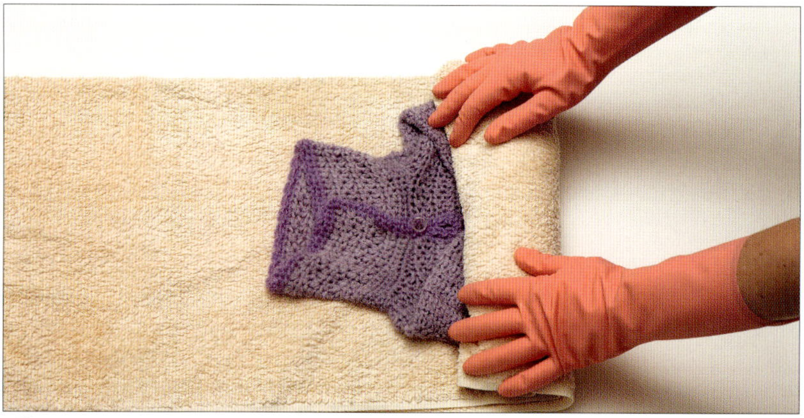

2 Roll the crochet in a towel to blot away excess moisture (never use a spin or tumble dryer).

3 Lay the crochet flat on a clean towel and pat it into shape. Leave it in a warm place, away from direct sunlight, to dry completely.

How to press

Consult the ball band: some ball bands recommend pressing under a dry cloth and others, a damp cloth, for steam. If a damp cloth is required, wring out a clean cotton cloth in cold water until it is just damp (not wet). If in doubt about the suitability of pressing, use your tension sample as a test piece.

For best results, press crochet pieces before assembling your project. After assembly, seams may be gently pressed to improve their appearance.

1 Pin the crochet on a blocking board, wrong-side down, flat and square. (Small pieces may be pinned out on an ironing board.) Check the measurements as you pin. Use large-headed pins at right angles to the edges, about 2.5–5cm (1–2in) apart, all around the edge of the work.

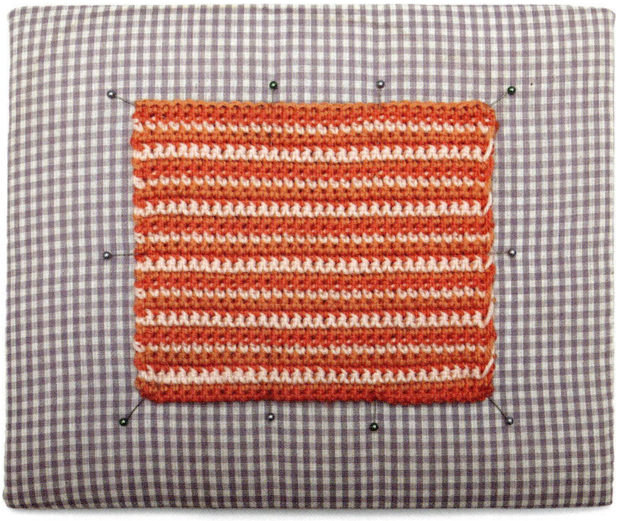

2 Heat the iron to the recommended temperature. If in doubt, begin with a cool setting, and increase the temperature gradually if necessary. Lay the dry or damp cloth over the work and hold the iron gently on the surface. Do not press hard down. Do not move the iron around on the surface, but lift and replace it to treat the whole area. Remove the cloth and leave the work to cool and/or dry completely before unpinning it.

HOW TO MAKE A BLOCKING BOARD

- A special board, as shown at left, is very useful for pinning out pieces for blocking or pressing. About 60 x 90cm (24 x 36in) is a useful size. Make a blocking board by covering a piece of plywood or medium-density fibreboard with a layer of wadding, then a top layer of cotton fabric, folded over the edges and stapled to the back. Gingham fabric provides an instant grid for pinning straight edges and square corners.
- Small crochet pieces that need to be an exact size may be washed as at left, then pinned out to the size required on a blocking board, and left to dry.

Part 2:

Additions

Learn how to add those finishing touches that make a garment special: transform a simple design with a neat edging or border, a well-fitting collar or quirky pockets.

Adding edgings

There are two main types of edgings used for crochet: 'Grown-on' edgings (or edge treatments) are normally worked directly onto the edge of a piece of crochet. Borders are worked separately and sewn on. Neatly worked edgings of any kind help crochet articles to keep their shape – they prevent stretching, and stop edges from curling.

Grown-on edgings

Most grown-on edgings begin with a row of double crochet. Using a hook one size smaller than the recommended size for the edging yarn usually gives a good result.

Double crochet on a top edge

On the top edge of a main piece, work 1 dc in every stitch. If you are using a suitable yarn and hook, the edge should lie quite flat. If the edge buckles, try again working 2 dc tog at regular intervals to shorten the edge – if the edge puckers, try working 2 dc in the same place (or 1 dc, 1 ch) at intervals.

Double crochet on a lower edge

On a lower edge, work 1 dc in each base chain. Depending on the method used to work the first row of the main piece into the base chain (see page 13), insert the hook under one thread or two threads of the base chain. You can adjust the number of stitches in the same way as for a top edge, if necessary.

Double crochet on a side edge

On a side edge, insert the hook under two threads of the first or last stitch of each row. Work a short length (15cm/6in) to see if you need to adjust the number of stitches. Estimate the number of stitches according to these guidelines:

For double crochet: 1 dc in the side edge of each row.

For half-treble crochet: 3 dc in the side edge of every two rows.

For treble crochet: 2 dc in the side edge of each row.

For double treble crochet: 3 dc in the side edge of each row.

Double crochet at outward corners

At outward corners, work 3 dc (or 1 dc, 1 ch, 1 dc) in the same place, exactly on the corner.

Double crochet at inward corners

At inward corners, work 3 dc tog, with the central insertion exactly in the corner. Alternatively, work 2 dc tog, inserting the hook just before and just after the corner.

Further rows of double crochet

To work more rows of double crochet, turn the work in the usual way and work 1 ch, skip first dc, 1 dc in each dc, working 3 sts in centre dc of 3 at each outward corner and 2 or 3 sts together at each inward corner, as on the first row.

Working patterned edgings

Edgings may be added to your work in different patterns (see pages 66–77). Most require a particular number of stitches, so that the pattern repeat fits neatly along the edge.

Working grown-on edgings

Grown-on patterned edgings require a correct multiple of stitches in order to fit neatly.

Adjusting the number of stitches

The Small picot edging (see page 68) requires an odd number of stitches. Count the stitches as you work the row before the picot row, and if necessary work 2 dc tog just before the end of the row, in order to finish with an odd number of stitches.

Adjusting stitches for corners

Large edge patterns such as the Block edging (see page 72) shown here work better if the pattern repeat ends at a corner, then begins again on the next side. This pattern requires a multiple of 4 sts, plus 1, on each edge. Work a sample of edging before beginning, so that you understand the construction and the pattern repeat.

As you work the row before the final row, count the stitches carefully, from one corner stitch to the next, along each section of the edge. (On long edges, place pins as markers every 10 or 20 stitches as an aid to counting). As you approach each corner, adjust the number of stitches as before, so that the centre stitch of the corner increase completes the required total (in this case, a multiple of 4, plus 1). At the corner, begin counting again at the centre stitch.

When you work the final row, the number of stitches will be correct on each section of the edge.

Work in the round

Edgings are often worked in the round. Instructions for edgings worked in rows may usually be translated into rounds, although the final appearance will be subtly different.

Double crochet in the round

Join the yarn in an inconspicuous place (for example, at a sleeve seam). Work 1 ch, then 1 dc in each stitch or position, all around the edge. Finish the round with 1 ss into 1 ch at beginning of round. Further rounds of dc may be worked in the same way. The total number of stitches may be adjusted as at left, to suit a decorative edging.

EDGINGS WITH FASTENINGS

- Before you work an edging, take into account any fastenings that will be required.

- Buttonholes or button loops may be worked at the same time as an edging (see page 38–41).
- Tie fastenings (see page 37) may also be added in the course of working an edging.

Working borders

Some borders are worked sideways, beginning with a short side, and working to the length required. By working these as shown below, it is easy to adjust the edging to the correct length. Other borders are worked lengthways, beginning with a long foundation chain, instead of growing them on the crochet edge. They are then sewn in place in the same way as shown below.

Fitting a sideways border

1 Work the border to the length you think you need, but do not fasten off. Leave the working loop on a split ring (or a safety pin). Pin the border in place, stretching it just slightly to avoid buckling.

Butt the two edges together and join with a flat seam (see page 19) from the wrong side. (For a firmer finish, lap the edge of the main piece just over the border and backstitch with yarn to match the main piece.) Try to match the same number of main piece stitches (or rows) to each pattern repeat of the border. You may need to replace the pins if you find you have stretched the border too much or too little. At corners, gather the border slightly so that it sits neatly. Join the seam to within about 2.5cm (1in) of the end.

2 If necessary, you can then work a few more rows, or unravel a few rows, to match the required length exactly. Fasten off the border and complete the seam.

BEGINNING WITH A SIDEWAYS BORDER

- A sideways border may be used as a base for further rows. The border is worked first, to the required length, then stitches are picked up along the long, straight edge to work the main body of the piece.
- Work the required length of border. This Chain Loop border is shown on page 76. With right side facing, work in double crochet along the straight top edge, adjusting the number of stitches if necessary to suit a subsequent stitch pattern.
- Continue in the required stitch. The simple mesh stripe pattern shown below is a good stitch for a scarf or wrap.

MESH STRIPES

Requires an odd number of stitches or base chains.

Row 1: 1 ch, skip first ch from hook, 1 dc in next ch, 1 dc in each ch to end. (In the example above, this first row is worked into the edging, making an odd number of stitches).

Row 2: 4 ch, skip first 2 dc, * 1 tr in next dc, 1 ch, skip 1 dc, * repeat from * to * ending 1 tr in 1 ch.

Row 3: 1 ch, skip first tr, * 1 dc in ch-sp, 1 dc in tr, * repeat from * to * ending 1 dc under 4 ch, 1 dc in 3rd of 4 ch.

Repeat rows 2 and 3.

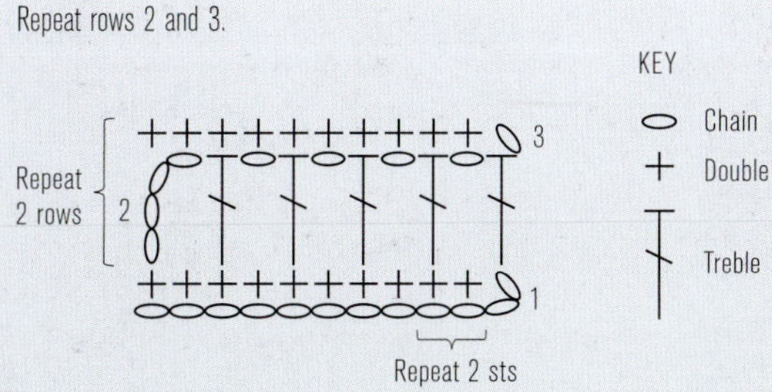

Collars

A neatly worked collar adds a professional finish to any crochet garment. Whether you are following a commercial pattern, or adapting a design by adding a collar to a round or V-shaped neckline, understanding the different ways in which collars may be formed will help you achieve the result you want.

This little jacket for a toddler has a neat fold-over collar, worked directly from the collar stand, making the collar 10cm (4in) deep at the back neck, and about 6cm (2 ½in) deep at the front.

Attaching a separate collar

A collar should be sewn on very neatly, as both sides of the stitching may be visible when the garment is worn with the collar up, or with buttons unfastened. A flat seam is best to avoid a bulky seam around the neck.

1 Fold the collar in half to find the centre, and pin this point to the centre back neck. Small safety pins are useful to hold the edges so that they meet without overlapping. Pin the front corners of collar and neckline together, matching exactly. Put in two or three more pins on each side, spreading both edges evenly.

2 Stitch with the right side of the main part of the garment (and the underneath of the collar) facing you. Thread a tapestry needle with a long length of matching yarn (shown here in pink for clarity), and begin at centre back, leaving half the yarn as a long tail. Use a flat seam (see page 19) to join the collar to the neck edge along from the centre to one front edge. Then use the long tail to join the other half of the seam, along to the other front edge. Remove the pins. Run in any yarn tails on the underneath of the collar.

GOLDEN RULES

- A collar may be worked separately, and then sewn onto the neck edge, or it may be worked directly outward from the neck edge.
- Whatever the method of working, the neck edge of the collar should match the neck edge of the garment (unless a frilled collar is required, when the collar edge may be longer, and gathered to fit the neck edge).
- Remember that a fold-over collar should be sewn on (or worked directly) so that the right side is uppermost when the collar folds over.
- Any border worked around the outer edge of a collar should not be tight; rather, it should be worked loosely enough to allow the edge of the collar to spread across the shoulders.
- For a neat fit, a classic fold-over collar often requires extra depth at the centre back neck. This is achieved by working a collar stand before attaching the collar, as shown over the page.

TIP

If the neck edge of the garment tends to spread after attaching a collar (or working a collar directly), crochet a row of firm slip stitch around the inside of the neck edge to keep it to the correct size.

Working a collar stand

A classic fold-over collar needs to be quite deep at the back neck – at least 10cm (4in) for an adult size – otherwise it will tend to stand upright instead of folding flat.

Straight collar

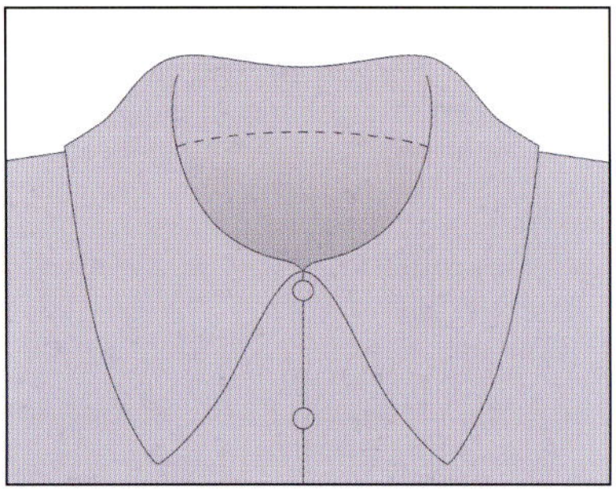

If the collar is the same depth all around, the front collar points will be relatively large.

Collar with a collar stand

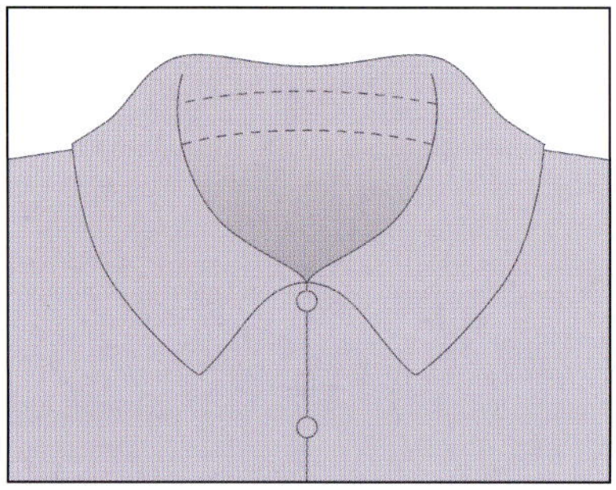

For smaller, neater, collar points it is necessary to add a collar stand to the neck edge before attaching or working the collar. This adds extra depth at the back of the neck only.

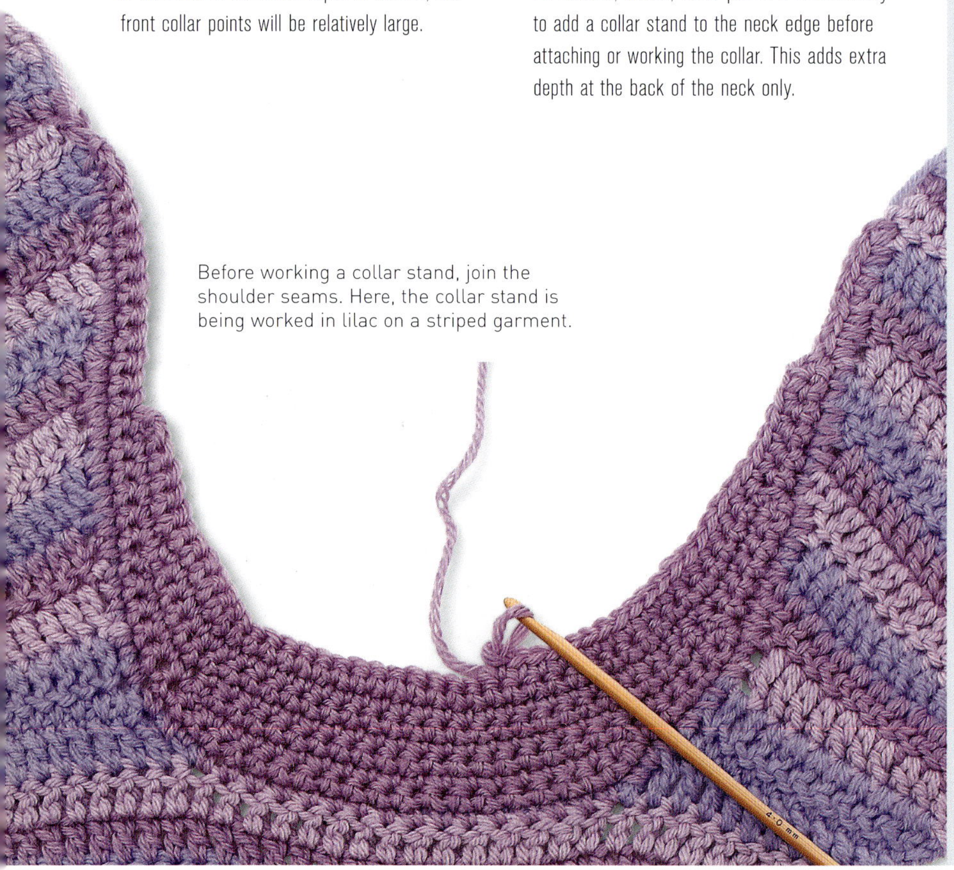

Before working a collar stand, join the shoulder seams. Here, the collar stand is being worked in lilac on a striped garment.

WORKING A COLLAR STAND IN DOUBLE CROCHET

Row 1: With the right side of the garment facing, join the yarn at the right front edge with 1 sl st, then work in dc (or as directed) all around the neck edge to the left front edge. (As a rule, work 1 st in the top of every st of the main part; on the side edges of the neck shaping, work 1, 2 or more sts in the side edge of every row, depending on the stitch pattern used. The neck edge should not be stretched or puckered by this first row.)

The collar stand is formed by working short rows, turning part way along each row to form a series of steps, making a curved edge about 2.5–5cm (1–2in) deep at centre back.

Count the number of stitches between the shoulder seam and the front neck edge (left and right sides should match). Divide these stitches into a number of steps: in this example, 8 short rows are needed for the extra depth at back neck, so there will be 4 steps on each side. There are 24 sts on each side of the front neck, making 4 steps of 6 sts on each side.

Row 2: 1 ch, 1 dc in each dc to second shoulder seam, turn.

Row 3: No turning chain. Skip first dc, 1 dc in each dc to first shoulder seam, turn.

Row 4: No turning chain. Skip first dc, 1 dc in each dc of previous row, 1 dc in same place as the last st of previous row (to avoid making a hole), then work the number of extra sts required for one step (6 in this example), turn.

Repeat row 4 until all the sts are back in work.

NOTE: If you are attaching a separate collar, fasten off. Otherwise, continue in rows for a grown-on collar, as opposite.

Working a collar onto a neck edge

A collar may also be 'grown' onto a neck edge. The example shown here is worked in rows, after working a collar stand.

The right side of the cardigan.

Working directly onto the neck edge

1 Begin by working a row of dc all around the neck edge, as for the collar stand, (see left). Then work the collar stand, if required.

2 Turn the work, and continue in pattern as desired. If the stitch pattern has a right and a wrong side, make sure that when the collar is folded over, the right side of the work will be uppermost. Work in rows to the depth required.

Pockets

Pockets are a useful addition to many garments (and accessories, such as tote bags). To be practical in use, the pocket should be large enough for the wearer's hand, and the stitch pattern must be fairly solid, with no large holes. Suitable crochet stitches generally make quite a thick fabric, therefore it is best to keep the construction simple by using one of the two basic methods: a slit pocket, or a patch pocket.

Slit pocket

For this pocket, a slit is formed in the main fabric, and a pocket lining sewn to the wrong side of the main piece.

1 Work the pocket lining before working the main piece. Use the same yarn and hook as the main piece to work a square or rectangle wide enough for the wearer's hand (20 stitches shown here).

2 On the main piece, work to the row required for the pocket slit. Work along the row to the position required. Then work along the top of the pocket lining instead of working into the main piece. On the main piece, skip the same number of stitches as the pocket lining, then complete the row on the main piece.

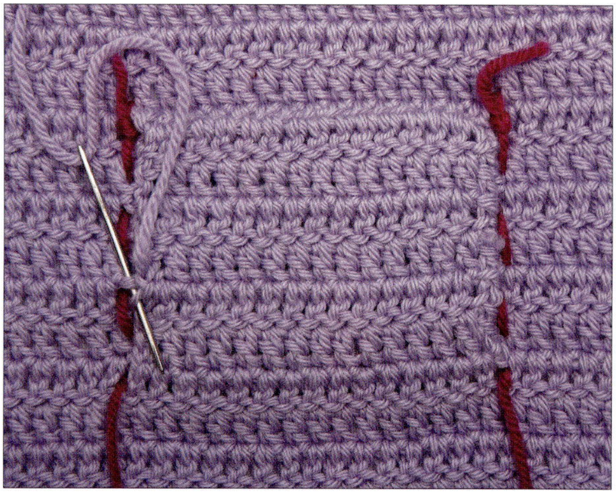

3 When the piece is complete, sew down the edges of the lining with matching yarn. To make sure the side edges follow straight lines of stitches, and the lower edge follows a straight row, you can first mark the required position with tacking, as shown in pink. Then use the overcast seam (see page 19) to sew down the edges, so the seam hardly shows on the right side of the work.

4 When complete, all that is visible on the right side is the slit. The slit may be edged with a row of double crochet as shown, or with a more decorative edging or border.

Patch pocket

A patch pocket is simply a square or rectangle of crochet, sewn to the right side of the main piece around three sides. Such a pocket may be quite plain, or used to add a decorative touch to an otherwise plain garment. A patch pocket may be added after the garment is completed, in whatever position you choose.

Diagonal block patch pocket

This diagonally worked square block is shown here in one colour, with a contrast edging, but could also be worked in stripes.

Begin with 4 ch.

Row 1: [1 tr, 2 ch, 2 tr] all into 4th ch from hook.

Row 2: 3 ch, skip first tr, 1 tr in next tr, [2 tr, 2 ch, 2 tr] into 2-ch sp, 1 tr in next tr, 1 tr into 3rd of 3 ch.

Row 3: 3 ch, skip first tr, 1 tr in each tr to centre, [2 tr, 2 ch, 2 tr] into 2-ch sp, 1 tr in each tr, ending 1 tr in 3rd of 3 ch.

Repeat row 3 until Pocket reaches the required size. Fasten off.

Using a contrast colour, work a Small Picot edging all around (see page 68).

Fold the starting corner over to make a flap and stitch it in place (add a decorative bead or button if you wish). Sew the pocket where required – this pocket is sewn on square, but you could also sew it on diagonally, with the folded edge matching a straight row of stitches.

Striped patch pocket with button

This double crochet patch is worked in three colour stripes (see page 49), with a buttonhole (see page 39) close to the top. The double crochet edging all around makes a neat finish. The patch is sewn in place by backstitching (see page 19) from the right side, through the double crochet edging, around three sides.

Flower block patch pocket

A square block like this one can make a lovely decorative pocket, but take care to choose a pattern without large holes.

Using colour A, 4 ch and join with ss to form a ring.

Round 1: 1 ch, [1 dc into ring, 3 ch] 8 times, 1 ss in first dc of round. Break off A.

Round 2: Join B to any 3-ch sp, 3 ch, [1 tr, 2 ch, 2 tr] into same sp, * 2 tr into next 3-ch sp, [2 tr, 2 ch, 2 tr] into next 3-ch sp, * rep from * to * twice more, 2 tr into next 3-ch sp, 1 ss in 3rd of 3 ch at beg of round. Break off B.

Round 3: Join C to any 2-ch corner sp, 3 ch, [2 tr, 3 ch, 3 tr] into same sp, * 2 tr in each sp between 2 groups to next corner, [3 tr, 3 ch, 3 tr] in 2-ch corner sp, * rep from * to * twice more, 2 tr in each sp between 2 groups to corner, 1 ss in 3rd of 3 ch at beg of round.

Round 4: 1 ch, 1 dc into same place, 1 dc in each dc and 3 dc in each corner sp all around, ending 1 ss into first sc. Break off C.

Round 5: Join D to any stitch. Work as Round 4. Fasten off.

Note: For a larger square, repeat Round 3.

Part 3:

Fastenings

Whatever type of fastening you choose, here's all the information you need for a professional finish: different methods of making and decorating tie fastenings, various types of buttonholes, choosing buttons (and making your own) and neat ways to sew in zippers.

Ties and drawstrings

Two lengths of crochet, cord or ribbon may be stitched where required and used as a fastening, perhaps to add a decorative touch at a neckline. To tie a reasonably sized bow, you need two ties at least 25cm (10in) long. Drawstrings may also be of crochet, cord or ribbon and are usually threaded through a row of eyelet holes. They may be used, for example, to gather the opening of a purse, or the waist of a garment.

Crochet chain ties

Depending on the yarn used, a simple length of chain may be suitable. The free end may be decorated with a bead, tassel, pompom or other suitable trim. Use the yarn tail to sew the tie in place.

Double crochet ties

For a more substantial tie, try this double crochet method: Working loosely, make a chain of the required length.
Work one row of double crochet into the back loops of the chain (see page 13). Fasten off.

Use the yarn tails to sew one end of the tie in place.

Again, the free end may be decorated if desired. The five-petal flower below is shown on page 82.

Braided ties

For a smooth, firm tie that will not stretch, take three lengths of yarn (or three groups, of two or more strands each) and braid them as you would braid hair.
If you start with six strands and double them, then braid them in pairs, the starting end of the braid will be a smooth loop that may be sewn where required. The other end is usually finished with an overhand knot and trimmed to form a little tassel.

Drawstrings

A crochet tie, braided tie or a length of cord or ribbon may be threaded through a row of eyelet holes to form a drawstring. For a crochet drawstring, choose a smooth yarn, that will not fray easily.

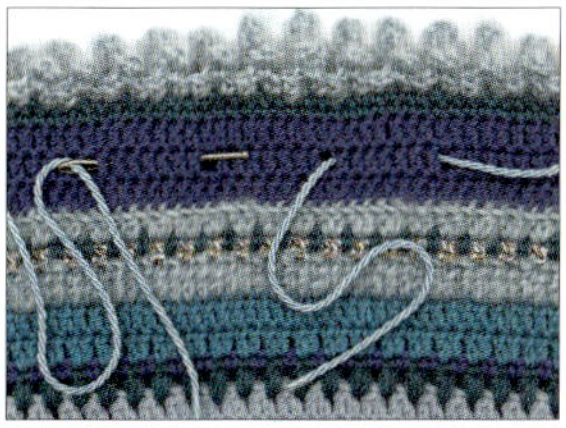

1 In order for the two ends of the drawstring to finish up on the same side of the work, ready to be fastened together, you need an even number of eyelet holes. To make an eyelet hole, simply work 1 ch, skip 1 stitch, then work into the next stitch. Space the eyelets evenly along the required row. Use a bodkin to thread the cord through the holes.

2 This little purse is threaded with two drawstrings, beginning at opposite sides of the purse. Each drawstring is joined into a continuous loop, by tying the ends together with an overhand knot, and trimming to form a little tassel.

Buttonholes

Neat buttonholes, when accurately placed, give your work a truly professional finish. It is a good idea to buy the buttons first – then you can make the buttonholes exactly the right size.

Spacing buttonholes

To space buttonholes accurately, for example on a jacket front, first complete the front that will take the buttons.

Mark the positions for the buttons on the button edge, with the same number of rows (or edging stitches) between the positions – use safety pins for accuracy. Then make the buttonhole edge to match, with holes to match the markers. For slits running parallel to the edge of the work, match the centres of the slits to the markers.

Sizing buttonholes

You need a stitch sample of the stitch you will use for the buttonhole area.

Lay your chosen button on the stitch sample and estimate the number of stitches (for a horizontal buttonhole), or rows (for a vertical buttonhole), needed to match the width of the button. Make one or two trial buttonholes on the stitch sample to ensure you are happy with the fit.

Working an eyelet buttonhole

The simplest buttonhole to work is the eyelet, which makes a hole suitable for a small button when worked in a firm fabric such as rows of double crochet or half treble crochet. In a more open stitch, this buttonhole requires edging with embroidery, otherwise it can prove difficult to find when fastening up a garment.

1 Work to the position required for the eyelet, work 1 chain, skip 1 stitch, then complete the row.

2 On the following row, work 1 stitch into the 1-chain space.

Horizontal buttonhole on a narrow edging

This buttonhole is used on a two-row edging worked in a firm, shallow stitch such as double crochet. On a jacket, for example, the slits will run vertically up the front of the garment.

Work to the position required for the slit, then work a number of chain (3 shown here), and skip the same number of stitches, before completing the row.

Horizontal buttonhole on a wider edging

Where an edging consists of several rows of double or half treble crochet, a firmer buttonhole may be worked on the centre two rows, as follows:

1 Work the edging to 1 row before half the total edging depth required (2 rows shown here). On the next row, work to the position required for the slit, then work a number of chain (4 shown here), and skip the same number of stitches, before completing the row.

2 On the next row, reinforce the corners by working 2 stitches together at each end of the slit as follows: work to the beginning of the chain, then work 2 stitches together, inserting the hook into the same place as the last stitch, and into the chain space.

3 Into the chain space, work the same number of stitches as the chains, minus two. Then work 2 stitches together, inserting the hook into the chain space, and into the next stitch. Work 1 stitch into the same place as the last insertion. The total number of stitches remains the same. Complete the edging.

Horizontal buttonhole in trebles or double trebles

When working in a tall stitch, such as rows of treble or double treble crochet, this method makes a narrow horizontal slit between two rows.

1 At the required position, work a number of extended stitches in the same way as shown on page 15 for a Step increase at the end of a row.

2 Skip the same number of stitches of the previous row before continuing along the row.

3 Complete the row as required. This buttonhole normally requires strengthening with embroidery such as chain stitch, or with slip stitch edging worked all around, as shown below.

From left to right: Eyelet buttonholes may be left as worked (above), or strengthened with embroidery (below); Horizontal buttonholes on a narrow edging; Horizontal buttonholes on a wider edging; Horizontal buttonholes worked in trebles (above), and strengthened with slip stitch (below).

Vertical buttonhole

A vertical slit is formed by working in two separate sections for several rows.

1 On the required row, work to the position of the slit, then turn and work further rows on this section only, to the required depth. Fasten off the yarn.

2 Rejoin the yarn at the base of the slit and work the same number of rows on the second section. (Make sure the first row is worked in the same direction as the first row of the first section.)

3 If the depth is an odd number of rows, close the slit by working across the second section, then the first. (If the depth is an even number of rows, fasten off the second section, rejoin the yarn at right of the first, and work across the first section, then the second.)

Buttonhole loops

These are normally worked when adding an edging, which may be only one or two rows deep. They are shown here worked on an edging of 1 row of double crochet. Loops may be any size required. This buttonhole may require strengthening with embroidery, or with a double crochet edging, as shown below.

Plain closed loop

For a closed loop as shown below, insert the hook back just one stitch along the row to close the loop of chains. Work double crochet into the chain loop as before.

Plain open loop

1 Work to the position required for the loop. Work a number of chain (seven shown here), then insert the hook a few stitches back along the row and make 1 slip stitch.

2 Work a number of dc into the chain loop until it is tightly covered (for a loop of 7 ch, work 10 or 12 dc). Work 2 dc tog, inserting the hook first into the last dc made on the edge, then into the next position along the edge. Complete the edging.

Button loop variations

Instead of a plain button loop, try these decorative variations when working into the loop of chains – add picots for a pretty embellishment or work a sequence of longer stitches to elongate the shape.

Oval loop

Work the loop of chains as for a plain closed loop (see left). Then work 2 sc, 3 htr, 5 tr, 3 htr, 2 sc into the loop before completing the edging as before. The numbers of double crochet, half-trebles and trebles may be adjusted to suit the size of the loop.

Picot loop

Work the loop of chains as given for a plain loop (see left). Then work [2 sc into loop, 3-ch picot] as many times as required, 2 sc into loop, and complete as for the plain loop. See page 116 for how to work picots.

Decorative buttonholes

Buttonholes and button loops may be decorated in various ways.

Frilly flower buttonhole

This flower is worked on a large eyelet hole, made by working 2 ch, skip 2 sts on the first row, and by working 2 sts into the ch sp on the second row.

Round 1: Using a second colour, work in sc around the edge of the hole (about 2 sts on each side, making 8 dc in all) and close with 1 ss into first dc made.

Round 2: 1 ch, 2 dc in each dc all around, ending 1 ss into first dc of round. Fasten off.

Round 3: Join a third colour to any dc. Work 3 ch, then 3 tr into each dc all around, ending 1 ss into 3rd of 3 ch at beginning of round. Fasten off.

Little flower button loop

On a double crochet or other edging, work a closed loop of 5 ch where required.

Round 1: 10 dc into the loop and join with 1 ss into the first dc made. Complete the edging as required.

Round 2: Join another colour to any double crochet on the loop, 1 ch, *1 dc into centre of ring, 2 ch, [2 tr tog, 2 ch, 1 ss] in next dc, * repeat from * to * 4 more times, 1 ss into first dc of round, fasten off.

From left to right: Vertical buttonholes may be left as worked (above) or strengthened with embroidery (below); Plain open loop (above), Plain closed loop (below); Picot loop (above), Oval loop (below); Little flower button loop (above), Frilly flower buttonhole (below).

Buttons

Choose buttons to suit your project: for baby garments, choose small, flat buttons; for adult garments, or an accessory such as a purse, you can make a feature of one or more large decorative buttons. To sew on buttons, use a sharp needle and matching yarn, or sewing thread in a matching or contrasting colour.

Buttons with shanks

These buttons have a little stem (called a shank) on the wrong side, with a hole through it for attachment.

1 Thread the needle with about 60cm (24in) of thread and tie the ends together. Pass the needle through the crochet, then through the knotted loop. Pull through.

2 Hold the button in place and make several stitches through the hole in the shank and the fabric. Pass the needle to the wrong side of the fabric and fasten off with two backstitches.

Two-hole buttons

For a neat appearance, position a two-hole button so that the holes line up with a vertical or horizontal slit buttonhole

1 Secure the thread as for the button with a shank (see left). Hold the button in position and bring the needle up through one hole, then down through the other, several times.

2 Bring the needle up through the crochet and wind the thread tightly around the previous stitches several times to form a shank. Fasten off with two backstitches on the wrong side.

Four-hole buttons

The usual way to sew on four-hole buttons is with stitches arranged in a cross, as shown here. They make a firm, secure fastening.

1 Secure the thread as for a button with a shank (see left). Stitch up and down several times between diagonally opposite holes.

2 Then stitch between the other two holes, the same number of times. If required, make a thread shank in the same way as for a two-hole button (see left).

From left to right: Buttons with shanks; Two-hole buttons; Four-hole buttons; Bobble buttons; Ring buttons; Vintage and novelty buttons.

Make your own buttons

Can't find a button you like? Try crocheting your own buttons to match or contrast with any project. Choose a hard-wearing yarn, and use a smaller hook than the recommended size, so the crochet is really firm.

Bobble buttons

This method makes a small, spherical button. You will need a small amount of toy filling or shredded matching yarn to stuff the button.

1 Begin with a small circle (2 or 3 increasing rounds) in double crochet (see pages 118–119). Then work a further 2 or 3 rounds without increasing. Draw up the starting tail tightly to close the centre.

2 Roll up a small, firm ball of filling and hold it inside the button. Work 1 or 2 decreasing rounds (say, * 2dctog, 1 dc*, repeat from * to *). Then work another round of 2dctog all around. Add more filling if necessary. For a firmer button, use a bead or button instead of toy filling.

3 When only a few stitches remain on the final round, fasten off leaving an 20cm (8in) tail. Thread the tail into a yarn needle and pass it through each stitch of the last round. Draw up tightly and backstitch to secure. Use the tail to sew the button in place.

Ring buttons

You will need a small plastic or metal ring.

1 Leaving a starting tail of about 20cm (8in), work a small circle of crochet to fit easily inside the ring. Draw up the centre by pulling on the starting tail but do not trim it off.

2 Then work another round into the circle, working over the ring at the same time. Fasten off securely and run in this tail. Use the starting tail to sew the button in place.

VINTAGE AND NOVELTY BUTTONS

- A button collection found in a charity shop can be a great bargain, and just one extraordinary button can even inspire a new project. However, some vintage buttons will not withstand dry-cleaning (or even machine washing), so always remove them before these processes, and sew them on again afterwards.
- Modern novelty buttons come in all shapes and sizes, and can add a unique touch to any project. Avoid shapes with sharp corners: choose smooth, rounded shapes like those shown below.

Zips

Zips make neat, secure fastenings for clothing, accessories and household items, such as pillows. They may be inserted unobtrusively into a seam or a slit opening, or emphasised as a decorative feature.

Inserting a zip into an opening

When assembling a project, an opening to suit a zip may be left in a seam, or the crochet may be worked with a slit (perhaps at a neckline), as shown below.

The opening should match the length of the zip from the top of the pull to the end stop – that is, not including the extra tape at each end. If preferred, the edges of the opening may be neatened with a double-crochet edging (see page 27) on each side, (as shown opposite for the open-ended zip), either to hide an untidy edge, or as a decorative feature.

1 Lay the zip on a flat surface, with the crochet opening on top, right side up. Match the crochet pattern at either side of the opening. The edges of the crochet should touch the zip teeth on each side, not overlap them, or they may become caught in the zip. Pin the zip tapes in place along each side, then tack with contrasting sewing thread.

2 Use sewing thread matching the crochet to backstitch down one side of the zip. Stitch through the edge of the crochet, spacing the stitches a little apart – for example, one backstitch per crochet stitch along a top edge, or about two backstitches to the end of one row of trebles on a side edge. Backstitch across the bottom of the zip and up the other side. (For a zip totally enclosed in a seam, backstitch across the top too, just above the pull.)

3 On the wrong side, slip stitch the edges of the tapes to the wrong side of the crochet, without stitching through to the right side. If the top of the zip ends at an edge such as a neckline, fold the ends of the tape under as shown and slip stitch them in place.

Inserting an open-ended zip

Open-ended zips are often used to fasten garments such as jackets. A double-crochet edging (see page 27), as shown here, makes a neat, firm edge to the crochet.

1 With the zip closed, pin in place in the same way as for a zip in an opening, shown opposite. The top of the zip should be flush with the neckline, and the tape ends folded under, as above. The lower end of the zip may be flush with the lower edge, or a short distance above it, as shown here.

2 Separate the two halves of the zip, tack and backstitch as before along each side, making one backstitch through the top of every stitch of the edging. Slip stitch the tape edges on the wrong side as before.

CHOOSING ZIPS

Choose the type of zip to suit your purpose, and the weight of your crochet fabric:

- Lightweight dress zips, for clothing and accessories in lightweight yarns.
- Medium-weight zips, for articles in medium weight yarns.
- Heavy-weight zips, for household articles and chunky outerwear.
- Choose the correct length – crochet should never be stretched to fit a zip.
- Choose a colour to match the crochet. If in doubt, a darker shade usually looks better than a lighter shade.
- Use a sharp sewing needle and sewing thread to match the crochet, to sew the zip in place.

DECORATIVE TOUCHES

Make a feature of a zip by sewing a crochet button (see page 43), a large bead or other decoration to the zip pull. Avoid trimming zips with tassels, pompoms or anything likely to catch in the zip teeth.

Part 4:

Creative touches

In this section you will find lots of exciting crochet techniques to explore: combining yarns, stripes, filet crochet, woven crochet, surface crochet, adding beads, embroidery, picture crochet and felting. Try them out to see where they lead you.

Combining yarns

Two (or more) yarns may be crocheted together to produce bold or subtle effects of colour and texture. There is no need to wind the two yarns together into a ball. Both yarns should flow freely, so that one is not tighter than the other. To achieve this, if possible pull each yarn from the centre of the ball. Otherwise, unwind plenty of yarn from each ball before working a row.

Tweed effect

This sample shows pale pink double knitting wool, crocheted together with dark pink 4-ply wool. The different shades of pink give a tweedy effect. This combination of weights makes an approximate equivalent to aran weight.

Combining yarn and thread

Sewing threads and fine embroidery threads can be combined with yarns for various colour effects. This sample shows pale pink double knitting wool combined with blue metallic machine embroidery thread (top), and with red/pink/orange shade-dyed sewing cotton (bottom). Combining a yarn with a very fine thread does not substantially affect its weight.

Blending colours

Here, two strands of 4-ply cotton yarn have been combined: one strand is pink and the other is coral. Because the two shades are quite close, they blend together to make a rich, subtle colour.

EQUIVALENT WEIGHTS

- Two strands of 4-ply are roughly equal to double knitting.
- Two strands of double knitting are roughly equal to aran weight.
- Two strands of aran weight are roughly equal to chunky weight.

USING SPOOLED YARNS AND THREADS

- Some fine yarns are wound onto card or plastic spools, and can roll off along the floor and around the furniture as you work. Put the spool into a small plastic bag and secure the neck of the bag loosely with a rubber band. Lead the thread end out through the opening. The same trick works with spools of sewing thread.

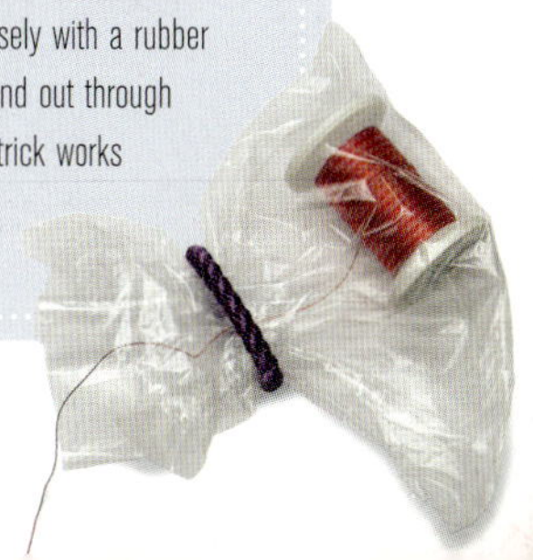

Fun with stripes

Stripes are a great way to add a splash of colour to a plain garment. There are several tricks you can use to avoid leaving lots of yarn tails and untidy edges. The techniques here are shown in double crochet, but they can also be applied to other stitches such as rows of trebles or double trebles, and also to more decorative stitches (see pages

Simple stripes

For repeating stripes in two colours, making each stripe an even number of rows (e.g. two rows, four rows) deep means that the colours can be stranded up one side edge of the work, thus avoiding lots of yarn tails. The strands may later be hidden within a seam, or enclosed by an edging. The sample shown below is in double crochet.

To change colours at the side edge, work to the last 'yarn round hook, pull through' of the last stitch. Join in the second colour, leaving a 10cm (4in) tail, and complete the last stitch. Do not cut the first colour, but leave it hanging. Work the next 2 rows with the second colour, up to the last 'yarn round hook, pull through' of the last stitch. Pick up the first colour, gently tightening the stitch below, and use it to complete the last stitch as before. Do not pull too tightly or the edge will pucker. Leave the second colour hanging. Continue in this way, changing colours at the end of every alternate row.

Isolated single-row stripes

To make a one-row stripe, it is necessary to fasten off and join in the colours.

1 At the end of a row in the background colour (pink), change to the contrast colour to complete the last stitch, as for Simple stripes, left. Cut the background colour leaving a 10cm (4in) tail. Depending on the stitch in use, you may be able to enclose both the tails within the next row – otherwise, leave them to be darned in later (see page 18).

2 Work one row in the contrast colour, changing to the background colour to complete the last stitch, as before. Continue in the background colour.

Repeating single-row stripes

For this stitch pattern, two right-side rows of double crochet (one in each colour) are followed by two wrong-side rows (one in each colour), making an interesting ridged texture. The same principle can be applied to rows of half trebles, trebles or double trebles. You will need a stitch holder (see page 9).

1 * Work 1 row in the 1st colour. Slip the working loop from the hook onto the stitch holder. Do not turn the work. Return to the beginning of the row, join the 2nd colour to the top of the first stitch with 1ss, work any turning chains required, and work another row in the 2nd colour.

2 At the end of this second row, work into the loop from the holder together with the last stitch. Complete the last stitch up to the final 'yarn round hook, pull through', then leave the 2nd colour aside and use the 1st colour to complete the stitch. Turn the work. * Repeat from * to *. Note that the work is only turned every 2 rows.

Single-row stripes in three colours

When working with an odd number of colours (such as three or five) it is possible to strand the yarns up the side edges of the work, thus avoiding breaking off and joining in the colours.

1 Work one row in the 1st colour, changing to the 2nd colour for the final 'yarn round hook, pull through' of the row, as shown for Simple stripes (see opposite). Work one row in the 2nd colour, changing to the 3rd colour at the end of the row as before.

2 Work 1 row in the 3rd colour. At the end of this row, the 1st colour is in position for the colour change. Continue working one row in each colour in sequence, stranding the colours quite loosely up the side edge of the work to prevent tight edges. The strands may later be enclosed in an edging or a seam.

From left to right: Simple stripes; Isolated single-row stripes; Repeating single-row stripes; and Single-row stripes in three colours.

Stitch patterns in stripes

The four techniques for working stripes on pages 48–49 can also be applied to many types of stitch patterns. A few examples are shown here, but it's easy to try out more.

Chevron pattern in three-colour, single-row stripes

The zigzag formation of the rows is enhanced by working Single-row stripes in three colours, (see page 49).

Using A, begin with a multiple of 8 ch, plus 4.

Row 1: 1 tr in 4th ch from hook, * 1 tr in each of next 2 ch, 2 tr tog over next and foll alt ch, 1 tr in each of next 2 ch, [1 tr, 1 ch, 1 tr] in next ch, * repeat from * to *, ending 2 tr in last ch, changing to B to complete last st.

Row 2: Using B, 3 ch, 1 tr in first tr, * 1 tr in each of next 2 tr, 2 tr tog over next and alt st (skipping top of previous 2 tr tog), 1 tr in each of next 2 tr, [1 tr, 1 ch, 1 tr] in 1-ch sp, * repeat from * to * working 2 tr in 3rd of 3 ch at end, changing to colour C to complete last st.

Repeat row 2, changing colours in sequence.

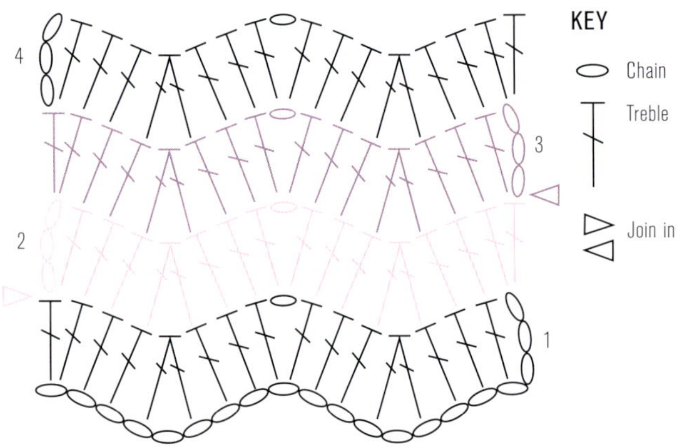

Close scallops in isolated stripes

For this scallop stitch sample, certain rows were worked as Isolated stripes (see page 48) in contrasting colours. Note the difference in appearance between the pink stripe (worked on wrong-side row) and the peach stripe (worked on right-side row).

Using A begin with a multiple of 6 ch, plus 2.

Row 1: 1 dc in 2nd ch from hook, * skip 2 ch, 5 tr in next ch, skip 2 ch, 1 dc in next ch, * repeat from * to * to end.

Row 2: 3 ch, 2 tr in first dc, * skip 2 tr, 1 dc in next tr (the 3rd tr of 5), skip 2 tr, 5 tr in dc, * repeat from * to *, ending 3 tr in last dc.

Row 3: 1 ch, 1 dc in first tr, * skip 2 tr, 5 tr in dc, skip 2 tr, 1 dc in next tr (the 3rd tr of 5), * repeat from * to *, working last dc into 3rd of 3 ch.

Repeat rows 2 and 3, introducing isolated stripes as desired.

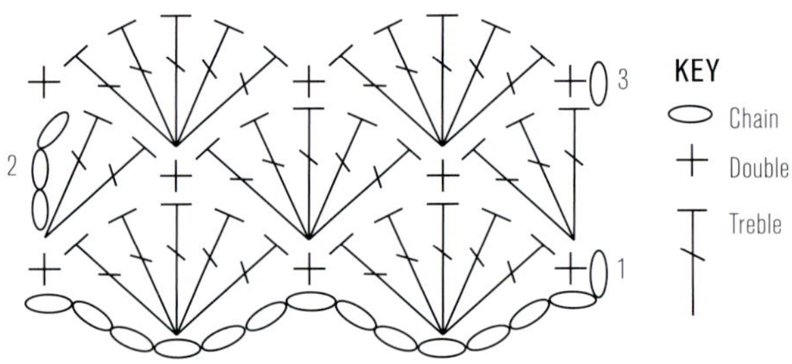

From left to right: Chevron pattern in three-colour, single-row stripes; Close scallops in isolated stripes; Big waves in simple stripes; and Rope stitch in repeating single-row stripes.

Big waves in simple stripes

This pattern repeats over four rows, so working Simple stripes (see page 48) of two rows A, two rows B emphasizes the pattern structure.

Using A, begin with a multiple of 8 ch, plus 2.

Row 1: 1 dc in 2nd ch from hook, 1 dc in next ch, * 1 htr in next ch, 1 tr in each of 3 ch, 1 htr in next ch, 1 dc in each of 3 ch, * repeat from * to *, ending 1 dc in each of last 2 ch.

Row 2: 1 ch, 1 dc in each of 2 dc, * 1 htr in htr, 1 tr in each of 3 tr, 1 htr in htr, 1 dc in each of 3 dc, * repeat from * to *, ending 1 dc in each of last 2 dc, changing to B to complete last stitch.

Row 3: Using B, 3 ch, skip 1st dc, 1 tr in next dc, * 1 htr in htr, 1 dc in each of 3 tr, 1 htr in htr, 1 tr in each of 3 dc * repeat from * to *, ending 1 tr in each of last 2 dc.

Row 4: 3 ch, skip first tr, 1 tr in next tr, * 1 htr in htr, 1 dc in each of 3 dc, 1 htr in htr, 1 tr in each of 3 tr, * repeat from * to *, ending 1 tr in tr, 1 tr in 3rd of 3 ch, changing to A to complete last stitch.

Row 5: Using A, 1 ch, 1 dc in first tr, 1 dc in next tr, * 1 htr in htr, 1 tr in each of 3 dc, 1 htr in htr, 1 dc in each of 3 tr, * repeat from * to *, ending 1 dc in tr, 1 dc in 3rd of 3 ch.

Repeat rows 2–5.

Try changing colours on rows 2 and 4 (instead of rows 3 and 5), for a quite different effect.

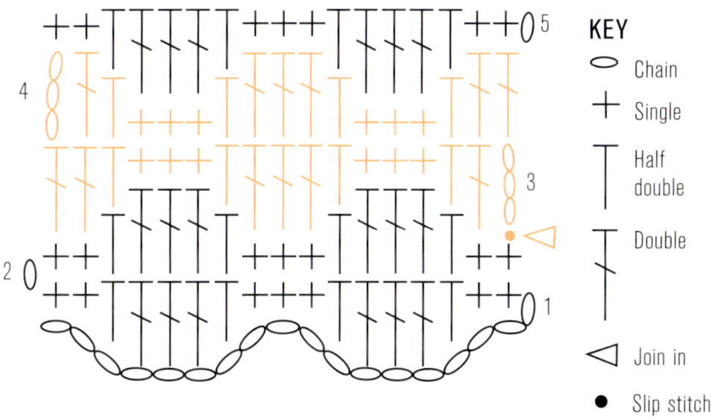

Rope stitch in repeating single-row stripes

This simple stitch pattern is changed to a zigzag effect by working in Single-row stripes in two colours (see page 49).

Using A, begin with a multiple of 3 ch.

Row 1: 1 tr in 4th ch from hook, * 1 ch, 1 tr in next ch, skip 1 ch, 1 tr in next ch, * repeat from * to * to last 2 ch, 1 ch, 1 tr in each of last 2 ch. Slip the working loop onto a stitch holder. Do not turn.

Row 2: Join B to 3rd of 3 ch at beg of row 1. 3 ch, skip first tr, * [1 tr, 1 ch, 1 tr] in 1-ch sp, skip 2 tr, * repeat from * to *, ending [1 tr, 1 ch, 1 tr] in last ch sp, 1 tr in [loop from holder tog with last tr], changing to A to complete last st. Turn the work.

Row 3: Using A, 3 ch, skip first tr, repeat * to * as for row 2, ending [1 tr, 1 ch, 1 tr] in last ch sp, 1 tr in 3rd of 3 ch, slip working loop onto stitch holder. Do not turn.

Row 4: Using B, 1 ss in 3rd of 3 ch at beg of row 3, work as row 2. Turn the work.

Row 5: Work as row 3.

Repeat rows 2–5.

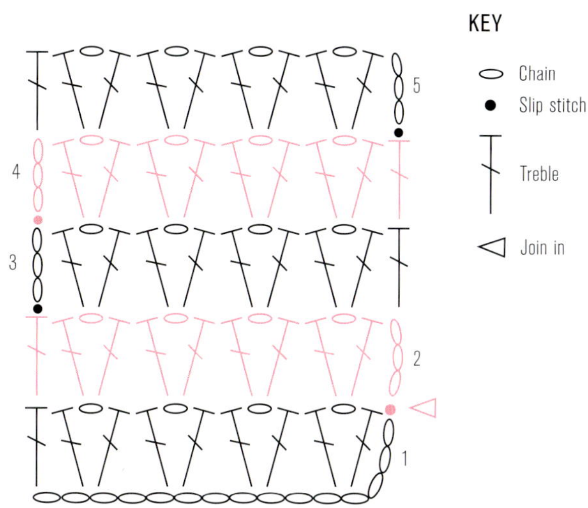

Filet crochet

The basis of filet crochet is a regular square mesh. Certain holes are filled with blocks of extra stitches to form a design or a repeating pattern.

Reading filet charts

Filet crochet designs are usually presented in the form of charts. Once the principle of forming 'spaces' and 'blocks' is understood, these charts are easy to follow.

Begin by following the bottom row (row 1) of the chart, reading from right to left (right-side row). Read the next row (row 2) from left to right (wrong-side row). Continue in this way to the top of the chart. On this chart, the row numbers are placed at the beginning of each row as a reminder of the direction of working.

It is a good idea to make a photocopy of a chart, then cross off each row as you complete it. Use pencil, so you can erase it if you want to use the chart again. An empty square on the chart represents a mesh 'space'. A filled square represents a 'block' of extra stitches.

Blue petal

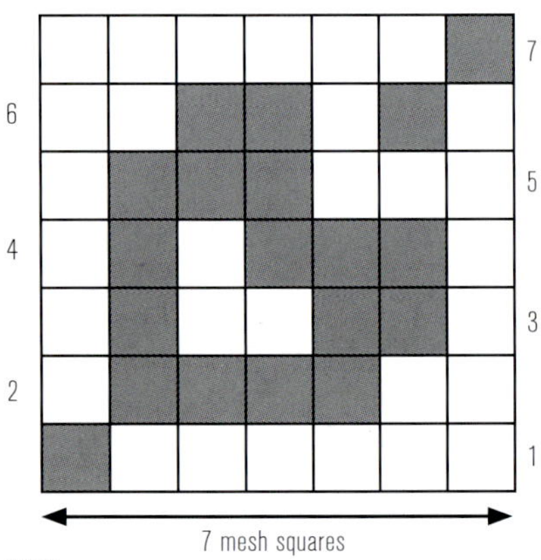

KEY

Space

Block

Basic filet mesh patterns

There are three basic meshes for filet crochet: small mesh, medium mesh and large mesh.

Small mesh

This basic mesh consists of treble crochet stitches separated by single chains. Blocks are formed by working one treble crochet instead of one chain. Depending on the hook/yarn combination used, this small mesh may give a rather indistinct result – a firm, smooth yarn gives the best definition.

Reading from the Blue Petal chart (see left), begin with a base chain of 2 sts for each chart square (14 ch for this chart).

Row 1: (*Reads 6 spaces, 1 block*): 3 ch to stand for first tr, 1 more ch for the top of the first space, 1 tr in 6th ch from hook (*first space made*), [1 ch, skip 1 ch, 1 tr in next ch] 5 times, (*5 more spaces made)*, 1 tr in each of next 2 ch (*1 block made*).

Row 2: (*Reads 1 space, 4 blocks, 2 spaces*): 3 ch to stand for first tr, skip last tr of previous row in the usual way, 1 ch, skip next st, 1 tr in next tr (*1 space made*), [1 tr in ch sp, 1 tr in next tr] 4 times (*4 blocks made*), [1 ch, skip 1 st, 1 tr in next tr] twice (*2 spaces made*). Work the last tr of the row into the 3rd of 3 turning chain at beginning of previous row.

Continue in this way reading from successive chart rows. After the initial 3 turning chain of any row, for a space work [1 ch, skip 1 st, 1 tr in next tr], and for a block, work [1 tr in next tr or ch sp, 1 tr in next tr].

Medium mesh

This is the classic filet mesh used for most traditional filet patterns, consisting of treble crochet stitches separated by two chains. For a block, the two chains are replaced by two treble crochet stitches. It is important to obtain correct tension (see page 6), so that the mesh is truly square – this mesh has a tendency to appear slightly squashed. Careful blocking (see pages 24–25) can solve this problem.

Reading from the Blue Petal chart (see opposite), begin with a base chain of 3 sts for each chart square (21 ch for this chart).

Row 1: (*Reads 6 spaces, 1 block*): 3 ch to stand for first tr, 2 more ch for the top of the first space, 1 tr in 8th ch from hook (*first space made*), [2 ch, skip 2 ch, 1 tr in next ch] 5 times, (*5 more spaces made*), 1 tr in each of next 3 ch (*1 block made*).

Row 2: (*Reads 1 space, 4 blocks, 2 spaces*): 3 ch to stand for first tr, skip last tr of previous row, 2 ch, skip next 2 sts, 1 tr in next tr (*1 space made*), [2 tr in 2-ch sp, 1 tr in next tr] 4 times (*4 blocks made*), [2 ch, skip 2 sts, 1 tr in next tr] twice (*2 spaces made*). Work the last tr of the row into the 3rd of 3 turning chain at beginning of previous row.

Continue in this way reading from successive chart rows. After the initial 3 turning chain of any row, for a space work [2 ch, skip 2 sts, 1 tr in next tr], and for a block, work [2 tr in next 2 tr or 2-ch sp, 1 tr in next tr].

Large mesh

Consisting of trebles separated by two chains, this mesh makes a more open fabric. The pattern definition is good, but the fabric is rather delicate and therefore not suitable for certain uses.

Reading from the Blue Petal chart (see opposite), begin with a base chain of 3 sts for each square (21 ch for this chart).

Row 1: (*Reads 6 spaces, 1 block*): 4 ch to stand for first dtr, 2 more ch for the top of the first space, 1 dtr in 9th ch from hook (*first space made*), [2 ch, skip 2 ch, 1 dtr in next ch] 5 times, (*5 more spaces made*), 1 dtr in each of next 2 ch (*1 block made*).

Row 2: (*Reads 1 space, 4 blocks, 2 spaces*): 4 ch to stand for first dtr, skip last dtr of previous row in the usual way, 2 ch, skip next 2 sts, 1 dtr in next dtr (*1 space made*), [2 dtr in 2-ch sp, 1 dtr in next dtr] 4 times (*4 blocks made*), [2 ch, skip 2 sts, 1 dtr in next dtr] twice (*2 spaces made*). Work the last dtr of the row into the 4th of 4 turning chain at beginning of previous row. Continue in this way reading from successive chart rows. After the initial 4 turning chain of any row, for a space work [2 ch, skip 2 sts, 1 dtr in next dtr], and for a block, work [2 dtr in next 2 dtr or 2-ch sp, 1 dtr in next dtr].

TIPS FOR SUCCESS

- For neat edges, take special care to always turn the work in the same direction at the end of each row (see page 13).
- If the mesh squares at the side edges appear unequal in size, try working one less (or one more) turning chain at the beginning of each row.
- A design worked in small or medium mesh can be incorporated into a project worked in rows of treble crochet – try a panel on a child's sweater or a tote bag. A design in large mesh can form part of a project worked in double trebles.

Woven crochet

Any of the three mesh patterns described on pages 52–53 may be used as the basis for woven crochet. Contrasting yarns may be woven through the open mesh to form striped or checked patterns. Woven crochet on small or medium mesh can make a firm, substantial fabric suitable for bags and soft furnishings. (See Tote bag, page 89).

Woven stripes

Lines of weaving in contrasting colours add interest to a plain crochet mesh, and make the crochet more stable.

1 To weave a straight line of holes, cut a length of contrasting yarn, the same length as the crochet plus about 20 per cent. Thread this into a yarn needle, and weave it in and out along the line of holes, leaving a tail of 10cm (4in) at each end.

2 Weave all the desired lines in the same way, then pat and gently stretch the work to settle the woven strands in place. The tails may then be knotted in pairs to form a fringe.

Woven checks

Lines of mesh holes may be woven in either direction, to form checked and tartan patterns.

The background of this woven sample is worked in a simple filet pattern from the chart below, with vertical and horizontal lines of mesh holes for the weaving (see pages 52–53).

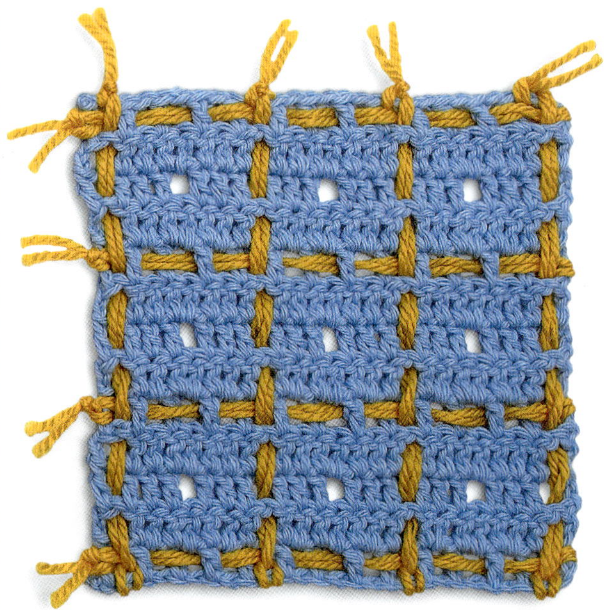

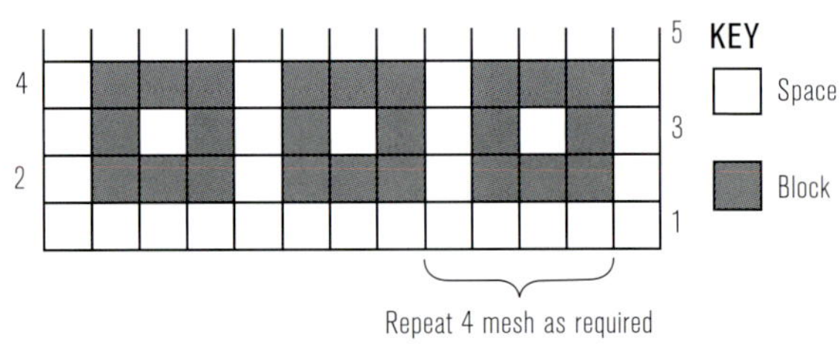

Surface crochet

This technique is often used to decorate a background fabric in small or medium mesh (see pages 52–53), although it can also be applied to other fabrics too. Lines of slip stitch (or other stitches) are worked through the background fabric. The lines may be straight or curved, making freehand designs of any formation.

Slip-stitch surface crochet

Work the crochet in small or medium mesh (see pages 50–51).

1 For a freehand design, cut a card or paper template and draw around it with an erasable pen (on dark colours, tack with sewing thread) to mark the required outline.

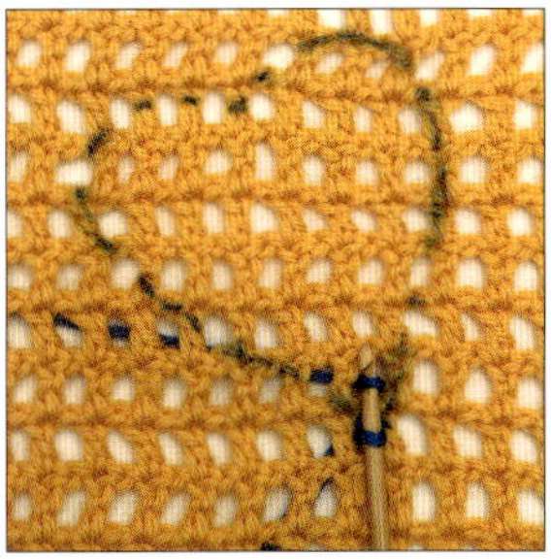

2 Begin with a slipknot in the usual way. Hold the yarn and slipknot behind the work. Push the hook through the crochet and through the knot, yrh, pull through a loop, making the first slip stitch. Work loosely in slip stitch along the marked line.

3 The yarn tails should be carefully darned in along the backs of the slip stitches so they will not show through on the right side of the work.

Alternative stitches

The background fabric need not be a filet mesh, as long as it is open enough to allow the hook to penetrate easily without splitting the yarn. The sample shown below is worked on offset mesh background, as shown on page 87:

1 To work in double crochet, treble crochet or other, longer stitches, the yarn must be held on the surface of the work (instead of behind it). This makes a heavier line than the slip stitch method. Begin with a slipknot on the hook, insert the hook through the crochet where required and work the stitch (treble crochet shown here).

2 The stem of this flower is worked in double crochet. The flower head is worked in treble crochet, placing the base of the stitches carefully in a circle, and working 2 trebles in each position. The centre of the flower is a bobble of 4 half trebles worked together into the same place.

Adding beads

The most secure way to attach beads to crochet is to work them in with the crochet stitches, rather than sewing them on afterwards. For this technique, the beads must have holes large enough to thread onto the crochet yarn (look for 'knitting beads'). The background fabric may be any pattern, but a plain stitch such as double or treble crochet shows off the beads to good advantage, and will hold them firmly in place.

Preparation

Before you begin the crochet, thread all the beads required onto the crochet yarn. If a needle threaded with the yarn will not pass through the beads, try using a finer 'leader thread' as shown.

Below, from left to right: Adding beads to double crochet; Adding beads to longer stitches; and Sequins, buttons and charms.

Adding beads to double crochet

The sample below is made in rows of double crochet. Beads are placed while working a wrong-side row, so that the bead rests on the right side of the work. Beads can be arranged in any pattern.

1 Work to the position required for the first bead. Slide a bead along the yarn so it sits against the right side of the work.

2 Work the next stitch tightly, catching the yarn beyond the bead. The bead sits on the right side of the stitch just made. Continue working stitches and placing beads as required.

Adding beads to longer stitches

Beads may also be added to longer stitches, such as trebles and double trebles. Again, they are placed on a wrong-side row.

Work the required stitch up to the last 'yrh, pull through'. Slide a bead along the yarn so that it rests against the front of the work. Catch the yarn beyond the bead and complete the stitch.

Sequins, buttons and charms

Other objects may be added to crochet in the same way as beads, provided they have a hole large enough to slide easily along the yarn. If a charm has a right and wrong side, thread it onto the yarn by inserting the needle from back to front. Large sequins, shanked buttons and various charms are shown, added to double treble crochet. Lightweight charms (such as the silver heart and gold flower basket shown) can be obtained from embroidery suppliers. Odd earrings can be used in the same way.

The necklace shown is very easy and quick to make. Thread about 100 beads onto fine yarn. Begin with a slipknot, then * work about 5 ch, place a bead *, repeat from * to * until all the beads are used up. Work 1 slip stitch into the first ch made. Fasten off.

Working from a chart

This chart represents the arrangement of beads shown on the second sample. Any bead pattern or motif can be charted in a similar way. The chart represents the right side of the work. Right-side rows (odd numbers) are read from right to left, and wrong-side rows (even numbers), where the beads are placed, from left to right.

Requires a multiple of 5 sts, plus 7

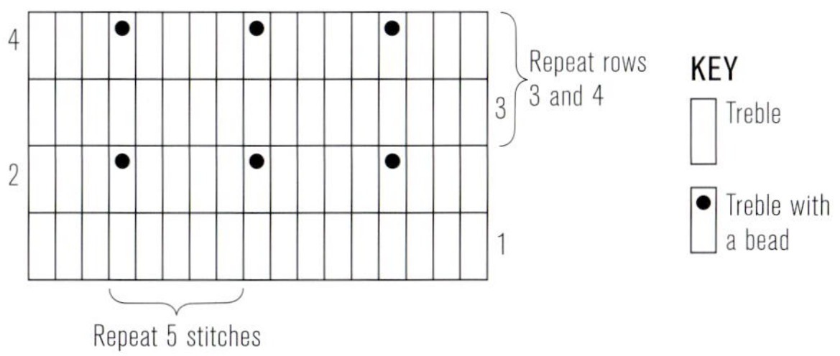

Adding beads to chain stitch

Beads can easily be added to a length of chain stitch at any intervals required.

Thread beads onto the yarn as shown opposite. Work a number of chains to the position required for a bead. Slide a bead along the yarn until it is tight against the hook, then catch the yarn beyond the bead to form the next chain stitch.

Embroidery

Embroidery can be used to personalise any simple crochet design – to add a single motif to the front of a child's sweater or add a border to a jacket. Four simple stitches are shown here, which can be used in myriad ways to enhance your crochet.

Materials

As a rule, choose yarn for embroidery that is the same weight as that used for the main project, or slightly heavier, and of the same fibre content (to avoid uneven shrinkage when washing).

If you don't have any suitable oddments of knitting/crochet yarns, you can purchase embroidery threads such as tapestry wool and soft cotton in small skeins – the range of colours available is huge. Choose a needle with a large eye that will easily take your chosen thread. Work with a length of thread no longer than about 50cm (20in). For working through stabiliser as shown, use a sharp-pointed needle. For working without stabilizer, a blunt-tipped needle will prevent split threads.

Chain stitch

Use this stitch for straight or curved lines and outlines, as shown on the butterfly, below. (The butterfly antennae are made with French knots with tails.)

Turn the work to embroider the line of chain stitch from right to left. Bring up the needle and form a loop with the thread. Take the needle down again where it emerged, and up inside the loop of thread. Pull through. Do not overtighten – the embroidery needs to flex with the crochet. Repeat as required. End a line of chain stitch with a small stitch to hold the last loop in place.

Single chain stitch

This stitch is often used for flower petals, and is therefore sometimes called 'lazy daisy stitch'. The flowers shown below are finished with a French knot (opposite) at their centers.

Make one chain stitch as at left, and fasten down the loop with a small stitch. Bring the needle up again where required for the next single chain stitch – you can pass the thread loosely across the wrong side of the work for 13mm (½in) or so, but for stitches any further apart it may be better to fasten off and start again.

French knot

This stitch may be used for flower centers. Groups of French knots can also form tiny flowers, as shown below. French knots can also be made with little tails (sometimes called pistil stitch).

1 Bring the needle up where required and pull the yarn through. Wind the yarn twice around the needle tip and holding it taut, insert the needle tip one crochet thread away from where it emerged.

2 Pull the needle through to the wrong side, gently tightening the knot. If you are embroidering isolated French knots, it is best to tie the two thread ends on the wrong side with a square knot and trim the tails to about 15mm (½in). Paint the square knot with anti-fray solution.

Blanket stitch

This stitch makes a decorative edging, or a spiky outline as shown on the heart, below.

Turn the work to embroider the line of blanket stitch from left to right. Bring the needle up on the lower line where required, form a loop with the thread. * Insert the needle on the top line, a short distance to the right and bring it out directly below, on the lower line, inside the loop. Pull through *. Repeat from * to * to the end of the line, fasten off with a small stitch over the last loop.

GENERAL GUIDELINES

- For simple designs, use the card template method described on page 55.
- For more intricate designs, trace the required design onto a piece of lightweight, non-fusible stabiliser (sold for dressmaking purposes), or a piece of tissue paper. Pin it where required to the right side of the crochet and tack all around with a small sharp needle and sewing thread. The embroidery can then be worked through both layers together.
- Thread a large, sharp needle with required yarn or thread. Make a small stitch through the stabiliser about 10cm (4in) away from the beginning of the embroidery, leaving a short tail on the surface. Take the needle through to the back, and bring it up again where required for the first embroidery stitch. Work the required embroidery, without catching the starting tail in the stitches.
- When the stitching is complete, take the thread through to the wrong side and darn it in, along the backs of the embroidery stitches. Unpick the backstitch at the beginning of the embroidery, pull the starting tail through to the back and darn it in as before.
- Remove the tacking and gently tear away the stabiliser or tissue. Small shreds may be removed with tweezers.

From left to right: Chain stitch; Single chain stitch; French knot; and Blanket stitch.

Picture crochet

Picture crochet (sometimes called 'intarsia') is a technique for working multicoloured, pictorial designs, using a separate ball of yarn for each area of colour. Designs are worked from charts, using basic stitches such as double, half-treble or treble crochet.

Reading charts

On this chart, each rectangle represents one half-treble stitch, and the proportions of the rectangles correspond to the proportions of half-trebles. (Charts from other sources may be drawn on a square grid, when the design will appear distorted).

The chart represents the right side of the work, so right-side rows (odd numbers) are read from right to left, and wrong-side rows (even numbers) are read from left to right. On this chart the row numbers are placed alternately to right and left to remind you of the direction of reading.

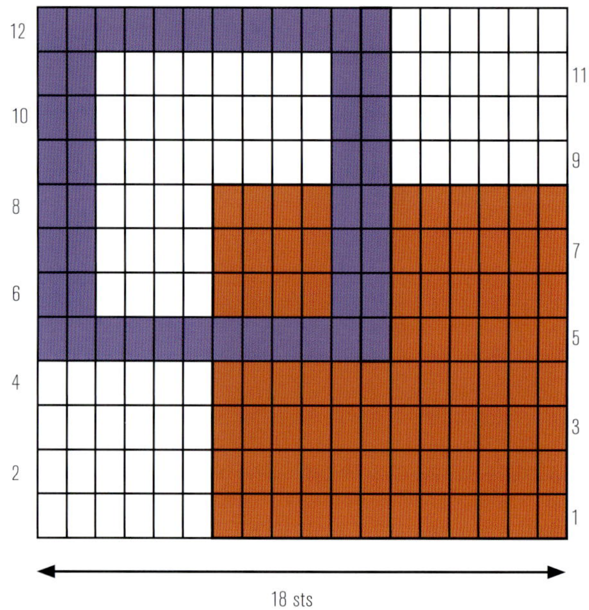

KEY

Background colour

Orange

Purple

Preparation

Prepare a separate ball of yarn for each area of colour. Centre-pull balls are less prone to tangling. Small amounts of different colours may be wound onto bobbins. Each separate area of colour requires a separate ball of yarn. For example, to place the design on the chart (left) on a sweater front, for chart row 1 you would need one ball of orange (for the orange square) and two balls of the background colour – one for the stitches to the right of the square, and one for the stitches to the left.

Working the first chart row

1 The Squares design charted at left is 18 half-trebles wide, and may be placed in any position required on a piece of crochet. It is a good idea to use marker threads, woven through the work on every row, to mark the edges of the charted area. Work to the row where you want the design to begin, then work the stitches to the right of the chart position. Take a length of smooth, contrasting yarn (shown here in white), pull one end through the next stitch to be worked, and tie a loose knot. Leave the long end at the back of the work.

2 At the position required for the first colour change, work the last stitch in the old colour up to the final 'yrh, pull through', then drop the old colour and use the new colour to complete this stitch, leaving a tail of about 10cm (4in) on the wrong side of the work.

3 Work the first row of the chart, joining in more new balls of different colours as required, then place a second marker thread. At the end of this row and every following row, turn the work in the usual way and untangle the balls of yarn.

On the following rows, when you reach a marker thread, pass it across to the other side of the work before working the next stitch. The two threads are woven in up a vertical line of stitches as work proceeds, marking the side edges of the charted area.

Note: If you are working from a large chart, or a chart showing the whole width of a crochet piece, it is often helpful to place marker threads every 10 or 20 stitches as an aid to accurate counting.

To change colours on a right-side row

Continue reading from the chart in position as set. To change from one colour to the next on a right-side row, work to the last 'yrh, pull through' of the last stitch in the old colour, then bring up the new colour behind the old colour to complete this stitch and continue. The two colours should cross on the wrong side of the work.

To change colours on a wrong-side row

To change colours on a wrong-side row, work to the last 'yrh, pull through' of the last stitch in the old colour, as before, then bring the yarn forward in front of the hook. Pick up the next colour (which should have been left on the wrong side, on the previous row), behind the old colour. Take it back in front of the hook, and use it to complete the stitch and continue. Again, the two colours cross on the wrong side of the work.

To enclose a colour across several stitches

Sometimes it is convenient to carry a colour across several stitches instead of joining in yet another ball. In our example, on chart row 5 (right side row), it is a good idea to carry the orange yarn across 6 purple stitches, to where it will be required on row 6. To avoid a long 'float' on the wrong side, enclose the orange yarn as you work the 6 purple stitches. The orange will not show because it is carried along the tops of the orange stitches of the row below.

Where practicable, yarn tails may be enclosed in the same way, to avoid having to darn them in later (see page 113).

To strand across a few stitches

On rows 6, 7 and 8 of our chart, the orange yarn should not be enclosed by the 2 purple stitches, because then it would probably show through on the right side. Simply carry the orange yarn across the wrong side of the work. Depending on the nature of the project, this method is usually fine if the resulting strand of orange yarn spans only two or three stitches. If the distance is greater, it is best to join in a separate ball to avoid long 'floats', which can catch on fingers, jewellery etc.

Another method of spanning several stitches is to leave an extra-long float, which can later be snipped at the centre, and the two tails darned in separately.

Finishing the picture

1 When the chart is complete, snip the unwanted colours leaving 10cm (4in) tails. Complete the crochet piece, then darn in any remaining ends along the backs of stitches of the same colour.

2 Untie the marker threads and pull them out.

Flower motif in double crochet

This flower chart is designed to be worked in double crochet – note the different proportions of the individual rectangles. The working method for double crochet is the same as in the previous example.

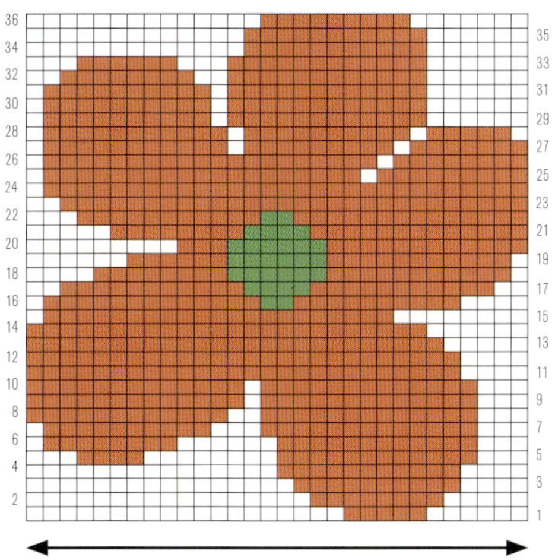

30 sts

KEY
- Background colour
- Orange
- Green

Monkey in treble crochet

This Monkey is worked in trebles, with details added later. The mouth is embroidered in chain stitch and the nostrils in French knots (see pages 58–59), and two black buttons are sewn on for the eyes (see pages 42–44). This motif could be added to a plain sweater (or other project) worked in trebles (see page 93).

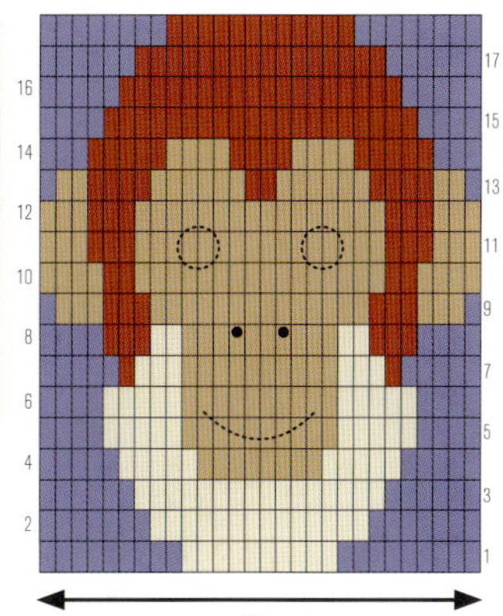

28 sts

KEY
- Background colour
- Natural white
- Light tan
- Rust
- Sew on button
- French knot in black
- Chain stitch in black

Felting

When woollen crochet is vigorously washed, the fibres mat together, and the crochet shrinks to form a sturdy, dense fabric suitable for pillows, rugs and bags.

Choosing yarns

Pure wool yarn is the best choice for felting – it should shrink by 25 per cent or more in the felting process. Other animal fibres, such as mohair, usually produce good results. Wool/synthetic blends may shrink to a lesser degree. Vegetable fibres such as cotton hardly shrink at all.

Loosely spun woollen yarns (such as Lopi and Shetland types) produce a dense, fuzzy fabric, in which the original stitches are almost indistinguishable. Yarns that are more tightly spun tend to retain more of the appearance of the crochet stitches. Yarns labeled 'machine-washable' have been specially treated to resist shrinkage and will therefore not felt satisfactorily.

Make some samples

Before beginning any felting project, it is always advisable to make one or more test pieces.

1 Make a tension swatch (see page 6) using your chosen yarn and stitch pattern. Make a note of the numbers of stitches and rows, the hook size, and the size of the swatch. This sample was made in aran-weight yarn of 85 per cent wool and 25 per cent mohair, worked in rows of trebles: 20 sts x 10 rows. Before felting, it measured 13.5 x 13.5cm (5¼ x 5¼in).

2 Put the swatch in the washing machine together with an old towel (or something similar) to add friction to the process. Set the machine for the longest, hottest wash (you can use a half-capacity program) and add the normal amount of detergent. After washing, dry the swatch flat.

3 Measure the swatch again. The felted sample shown measures 10 x 9.5cm (4 x 3¾in), so it has shrunk slightly more in the vertical direction: the rows have shrunk more than the stitches. So the new tension is 20 sts to 10cm (4in) and approximately 10 ½ rows to 10cm (4in). This shrunken tension measurement should be used when planning a felted project.

Before

After

Colour effects

Felting often also affects the yarn colours, as some of the dye may be washed out during the process. This striped sample was made in the same yarn as at left, in rows of double trebles. After felting, the colours are somewhat faded, and the edges of the stripes are blurred.

Before

After

Textural effects

Interesting effects can be obtained by using a shrinkable yarn together with a non-shrinkable yarn. These before-and-after samples were made using lilac wool and blue cotton double knitting yarns, in two-row stripes of Puff stitch. After felting, only the lilac wool stitches have shrunk, making a firm fabric with a pleasing crunchy texture.

Puff stitch

For details of how to change colours for stripes, see page 48. In the sample colour A is lilac wool, and colour B is blue cotton.

Using colour A, begin with a multiple of 4 ch, plus 3.

Row 1: 1 dc in 2nd ch from hook, 1 dc in each ch to end, changing to colour B at end of row.

Row 2: In B, 1 ch, skip first dc, 1 dc in each of 2 dc, * 4 htr tog in next dc, 1 dc in each of 3 dc, * repeat from * to * to end, working last dc in 1 ch at beg of previous row.

Row 3: 1 ch, skip first dc, 1 dc in each st, working last dc in 1 ch and changing to colour A at end of row.

Row 4: In A, 1 ch, skip first dc, 1 dc in each dc, working last dc in 1 ch.

Row 5: As row 4, changing to B at end of row.

Row 6: In B, 1 ch, skip first dc, * 4 htr tog in next dc, 1 dc in each of next 3 dc, * repeat from * to * to last 2 sts, 4 htr tog in next dc, 1 dc in 1 ch.

Row 7: As row 3.

Rows 8 and 9: In A, as row 4, changing to B at end of row 9. Repeat rows 2–9.

Before

After

Felting three-dimensional pieces

Felted wool is very tough, and suitable for articles such as toys, which may be assembled, felted and then stuffed with safety toy filling. Another method is to stuff the article with shredded wool before felting. Or construct your project from several layers of crochet, like this pincushion:

This little pincushion was made in chunky 100 per cent wool yarn, using a 5mm hook.

Use pale pink yarn to make 1 small and 2 large hearts, as page 85. Sandwich the small heart between the 2 large ones, and use dark pink yarn to work in double crochet all around the outside edge, joining the 2 large hearts together. Then work a Plain ruffle frill as given on page 71. Felt the pincushion using the washing machine method. While still damp, pull the frill into even folds, then leave to dry completely.

CONTROL THE SHRINKAGE

The washing-machine felting process described is rather drastic, and irreversible. You can obtain the exact amount of shrinkage you want by one of these methods:

- Use an old-fashioned top-loading washing machine. Stop the machine every couple of minutes and lift the crochet out with tongs to check the size, until it has shrunk to the dimensions you want. Rinse thoroughly in cool water and block the work to size (see page 25). Leave it to dry completely.
- For the second method, you will need something to rub the crochet with, such as a washboard (or try a piece of bubble-wrap), and also a nailbrush. Wear rubber gloves. Prepare a bowl of hot, soapy water and another of very cold water. Wash the crochet in the hot water for a couple of minutes, lift it out and rub it vigorously on the washboard or bubble-wrap, and brush it with the nailbrush to fluff up the fibres. Plunge it into the cold water. Repeat the hot/rub/cold cycle until the work has shrunk to the size you want. Rinse well and block to size (see page 25). Leave to dry.

Part 5:

Directory of edgings

From simple picots to bold fringing, a well-chosen edging can add the perfect finishing touch to a garment or other project. Browse here to find the look you want.

Crab stitch

Crab stitch is also known as corded edging, or reverse double crochet. Worked lengthways, this firm, twisted edging is usually used as a finish for one or more rows or rounds of double crochet. The method of working reverse double crochet is shown on page 116.

Work any number of sts, as required:
With right side of work facing, begin at right and work one or more rows or rounds of double crochet (see page 27), ending at left.
Crab stitch row: (chart row 2, worked from left to right), 1 ch, skip first dc, 1 reverse dc in each dc, ending 1 dc in 1 ch. Fasten off.

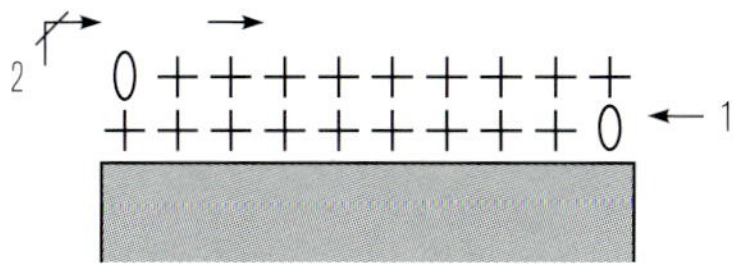

KEY

- ⬭ Chain
- + Double
- ↱ Do not turn
- ← Work right to left
- → Work left to right

Rope stitch

This variation on Crab stitch (see above) makes an edging with a looser twist. The method of working reverse double crochet is shown on page 116.

With right side of work facing, begin at right and work one or more rows or rounds of double crochet (see page 27), ending at left with an even number of stitches.
Rope stitch row: (chart row 2, worked from left to right), 2 ch, skip first dc, * 1 reverse dc in next dc to the right, 2 ch, skip 1 dc * repeat from * to *, working last dc in 1 ch. Fasten off.

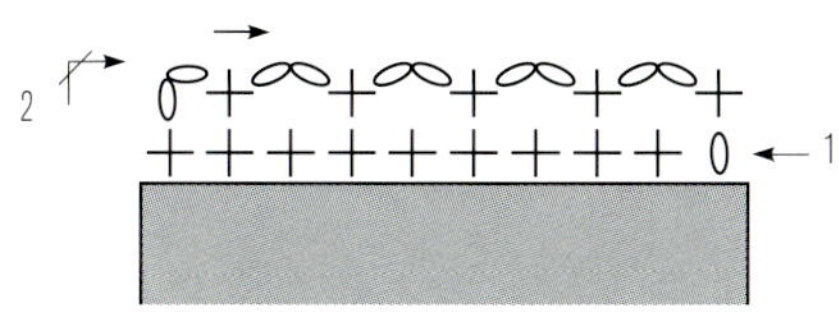

KEY

- + Double
- ↱ Do not turn
- ⬭ Chain
- ← Work right to left
- → Work left to right

Small picot edging

This edging is worked lengthways, usually as the final row of a double-crochet border (see page 27). For methods of working picots, see page 116.

With right side of work facing, begin at right and work an even number of rows of double crochet (see page 27), ending at right with an odd number of stitches.

Small picot row: (chart row 3) 1 ch, skip first dc, * 3 ch, 1 ss in first of these 3 ch, skip 1 dc, 1 dc in next dc, * repeat from * to * to end, working last dc in 1 ch. Fasten off.

Notes:

- At outward corners, try working [3 ch, 1 ss in first of these 3 ch, 1 dc in next dc] twice, exactly at the corner, to enable the edging to lie flat.
- At inward corners, work 2 (or 3) dc tog exactly in the corner.
- If working in rounds, any number of rounds of dc may precede the Small picot row.

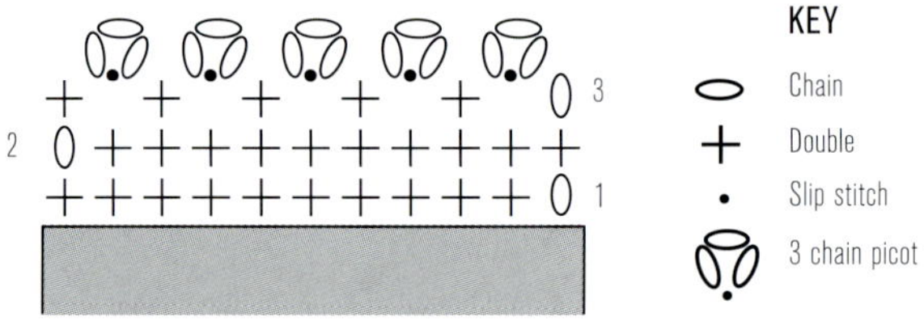

Large picot edging

This edging may be used as a substitute for Small picot edging, for a bolder effect. For more about picots, see page 116.

With right side of work facing, begin at right and work an even number of rows of double crochet (see page 27), ending at right with a multiple of 3 stitches, plus 2.

Large picot row: (chart row 3) 1 ch, skip first dc, 1 dc in next dc, * 5 ch, 1 ss in first of these 5 ch, skip 1 dc, 1 dc in each of next 2 dc, * repeat from * to * to end, working last dc in 1 ch. Fasten off.

Notes:

- As you approach an outward corner, adjust the number of stitches by working 2 dc tog once or twice at intervals if necessary, so that a picot will fall exactly on the corner.
- At inward corners, work 2 (or 3) dc tog exactly in the corner.
- If working in rounds, any number of rounds of dc may precede the Large Picot row.

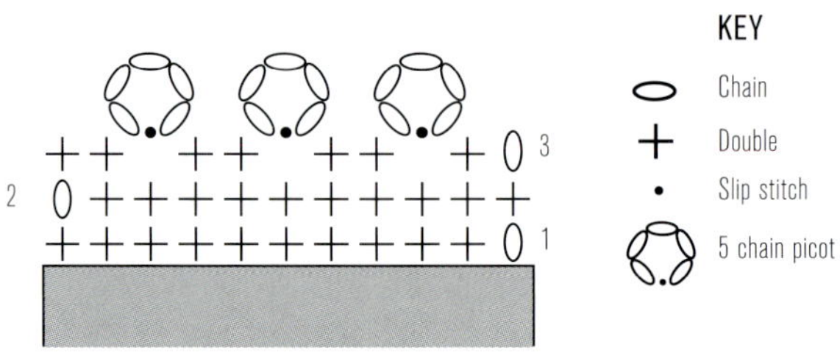

Crown picot

This edging may be used as a substitute for Small picot edging, for a bolder effect. Methods of working picots are shown on page 116.

With right side of work facing, begin at right and work an even number of rows of double crochet (see page 27), ending at right with a multiple of 5 stitches.

Crown picot row: (chart row 3) 1 ch, skip first dc, * [1ss, 4 ch,1 ss] in next dc, [1 ss, 3 ch, 1 dtr, 3 ch, 1 ss] in next dc, [1 ss, 4 ch, 1 ss] in next dc, 1 dc in each of next 2 dc, * repeat from * to *, ending 1 dc in 1 ch. Fasten off.

Notes:

- As you approach an outward corner, if necessary adjust the number of stitches by working 2 dc tog once or twice at intervals, so that the 2 dc between picots will fall on the corner (or so that the centre stitch of the picot will fall on the corner).
- At inward corners, work 2 (or 3) dc tog at corner.
- If working in rounds, any number of rounds of dc may precede the Large picot row.

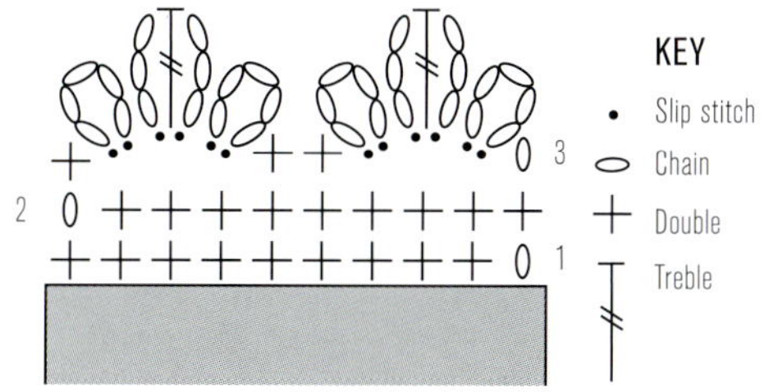

Shell edging

This pretty edging adds a delicate finish to a project in a plain stitch.

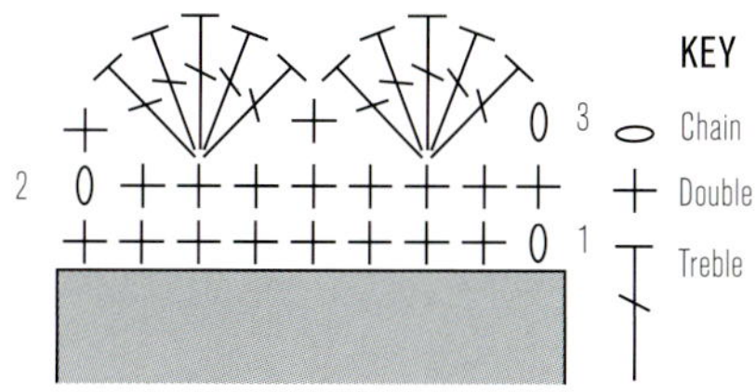

With right side of work facing, begin at right and work an even number of rows of double crochet (see page 27), ending at right with a multiple of 4 stitches, plus 1.

Shell row: (chart row 3) 1 ch, skip first dc, * skip 1 dc, 5 tr in next dc, skip 1 dc, 1 dc in next dc, * repeat from * to * to end, working last dc in 1 ch. Fasten off.

Notes:

- As you approach an outward corner, if necessary adjust the number of stitches by working 2 dc tog once or twice at intervals, so that the dc between two shells will fall exactly on the corner.
- At inward corners, work 2 (or 3) dc tog exactly in the corner, between two shells.
- If working in rounds, any number of rounds of dc may precede the Shell row.

Blanket edging

This one-row edging, worked lengthways, makes a firm, neat finish for blankets and throws. See page 117 for how to work spike stitches.

Work along the edge(s) required: on an upper or lower edge, work 1 st for each st of the edge; on side edges, space the stitches as for a double crochet edging (see page 27):

Row 1: Join the yarn where required, 1 ch, 1 dc in next position, * inserting hook at least 6mm (¼in) below next position, work 1 spike stitch, 1 dc in each of next 2 positions, * repeat from * to * to end. Fasten off.

Notes:

- The spacing may be adjusted by working more than 2 dc between spike stitches.
- On an outward corner, arrange the sts so that 3 spikes are worked into the same place, as shown. On an inward corner, fan the spikes out evenly around the corner.
- This edging may also be worked in the round.

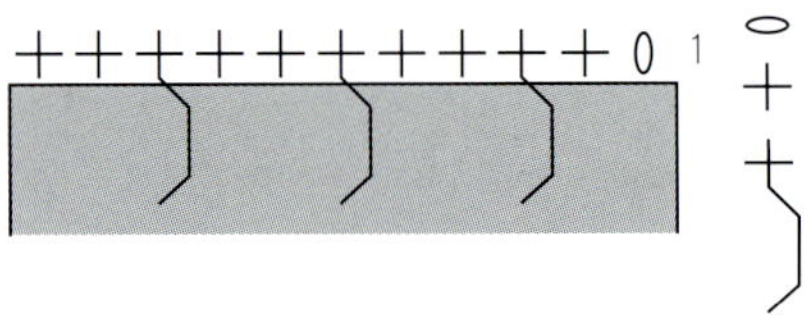

KEY

Chain

Double

Spike stitch

Spray edging

This edging is a variation of the basic blanket stitch, and stitches should be spaced in the same way as above. For the method of working spike stitches, see page 117.

Row 1: Join yarn where required, 1 ch, 1 dc in next position, * 2 spike sts tog, inserting hook in 2 places: [1st, below and right of working position; 2nd, below and left of working position]; 1 dc in each of next 3 positions, * repeat from * to * to end. Fasten off.

Notes:

- At outward corners, arrange the stitches so that sprays of spikes fall at the same distance either side of the corner – extra dc may be worked at the corner to achieve this. At inward corners, arrange sprays in a similar way, working 2 or 3 dc tog at the corner.
- This edging may also be worked in the round.

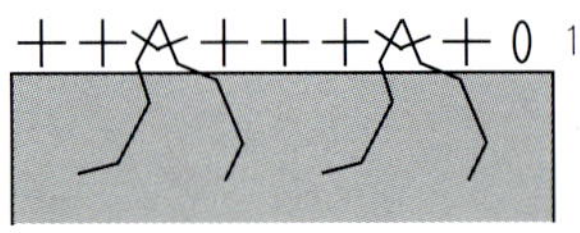

KEY

Chain

Double

2 spike stitches together

Plain ruffle

This edging is worked lengthways, and may begin with any number of stitches.

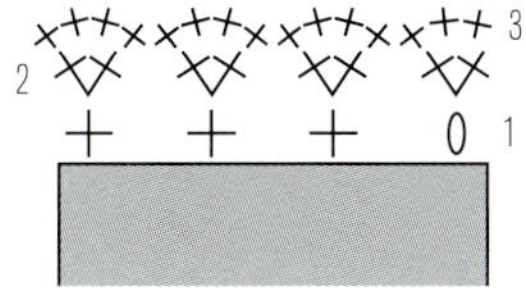

KEY

Chain

Double

With right side of work facing, begin at right and work 1 row of double crochet (see page 27).

Row 2: 1 ch, 1 dc in first dc, 2 dc in each dc, ending 2 dc in 1 ch.

Row 3: as row 2. Fasten off.

Notes:

- For a wider, looser ruffle work rows 2 and 3 in tr or dtr. For a tighter ruffle, repeat row 3 once more.
- At outward corners, work 3 dc in the same place on the first 2 rows of dc. At inward corners, work 3 dc tog on the first 2 rows of dc (see page 27).
- This ruffle is easily converted to working in rounds (see page 28).

Lacy ruffle

Worked sideways this pretty ruffle is easy to adjust to length (see page 29).

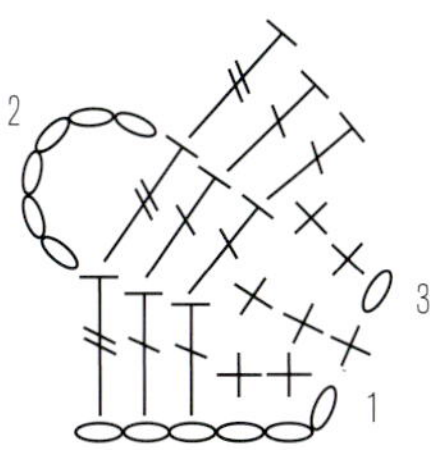

KEY

Chain

Double

Treble

Double treble

Work 6 ch.

Row 1: 1 dc in 2nd ch from hook, 1 dc in next ch, 1 tr in each of 2 ch, 1 tr in last ch.

Row 2: 6 ch, 1 tr in tr, 1 tr in each of 2 tr, 1 dc in each of 2 dc, 1 dc in 1 ch.

Row 3: 1 ch, skip first dc, 1 dc in each of 2 dc, 1 tr in each of 2 tr, 1 tr in tr.

Repeat rows 2 and 3 to required length, fasten off.

With right side facing, rejoin yarn at right of inside edge of ruffle and work in dc all along. This makes a neat edge to stitch in place.

Notes:

- At outward corners, gather the dc edging slightly to allow a little extra fullness.
- At inward corners, stretch the edge slightly as you sew it in place.

Block edging

Worked lengthways, this bold edging is quick and simple to work.

With right side of work facing, begin at right and work an even number of rows of double crochet (see page 27), ending at right with a multiple of 4 sts, plus 1.

Block row: (chart row 3) 3 ch, skip 3 dc, * 1 tr in next dc, 3 ch, 4 tr in sp behind tr just made, skip next 3 dc, * repeat from * to * to last dc, 3 ch, 1 ss in last st. Fasten off.

Notes:

- At outward corners, adjust the number of dc so that each edge has a multiple of 4 sts, plus 1 – the extra st should be the centre st of 3 at each corner (see page 28). On Block row, one tr (carrying a block) is worked into the centre dc of 3 at each corner.
- To work in rounds, work 2 or more rounds of dc (see page 27), ending with a multiple of 4 sts. Work 3rd round as Block row, ending 1 tr in base of 3 ch at beg of rd, 4 tr in sp behind tr just made. Fasten off.

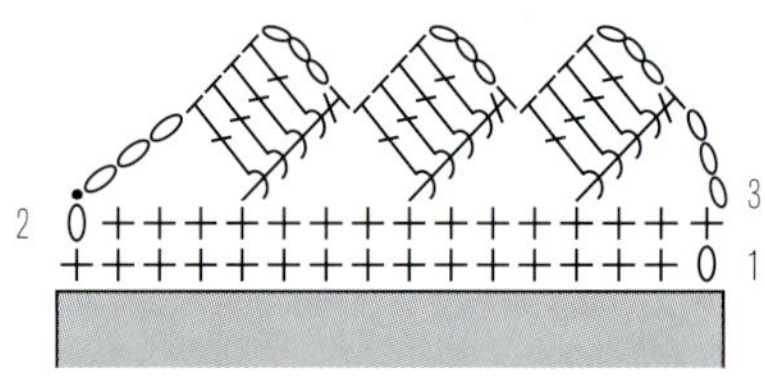

KEY

- Chain
- Slip stitch
- Double
- Treble
- Double around stem

Frilled flowers

This edging is worked sideways and sewn in place (see page 29).

Work 5 ch, join into a ring with 1 ss in first ch made.

Row 1: 3 ch, 7 tr into ring, turn.

Row 2: 3 ch, skip first tr, * [dc in next tr, 3 ch] 6 times, dc in 3rd of 3 ch, 9 ch, ss in 5th ch from hook (making another ring), turn.

Row 3: 3 ch, 7 tr into ring, 1 ch, 1 ss in last 3-ch loop of previous repeat, turn.

Row 4: 1 ch, work as row 2 from * to end.

Repeat rows 3 and 4 to required length, ending row 4 by omitting the final 9 ch and ss.

Notes:

- At outward corners, arrange the edging so that a join between 2 repeats falls exactly on the corner.
- At inward corners, work 14 ch instead of 9 ch on row 4, so that one repeat can be placed on either side of the corner.

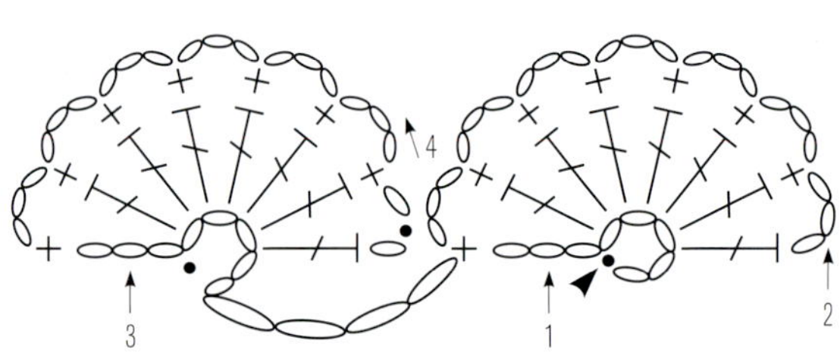

KEY

- Chain
- Slip stitch
- Double
- Treble
- Direction of work

Picot arches

This edging is worked lengthways, and is shown worked directly onto the edge of the main fabric. If preferred, begin by working 2 or more rows of dc, making a multiple of 5 dc.

Row 1: Join yarn where required, 1 ch, 1 dc in each of 2 sts or positions, * 5 ch, 1 ss in previous dc, 1 dc in each of 5 sts or positions, * repeat from * to *, ending 1 dc in each of 3 positions.

Row 2: 1 ch, * 3 ch, dc in next 5-ch picot, 3 ch, dc in centre dc of 5, * repeat from * to *, ending 1 dc in 1 ch.

Row 3: 1 ch, * 3 dc in 3-ch sp, 1 dc in dc, 5 ch, 1 ss in last dc made, 3 dc in 3-ch sp, 1 ss in next dc, * repeat from * to *, ending 1 ss in 1 ch. Fasten off.

Notes:

- At outward corners, adjust the stitches on row 1 so that the 3 centre dc of 5 dc are all worked into the same place at the corner.
- This edging may also be worked in rounds.

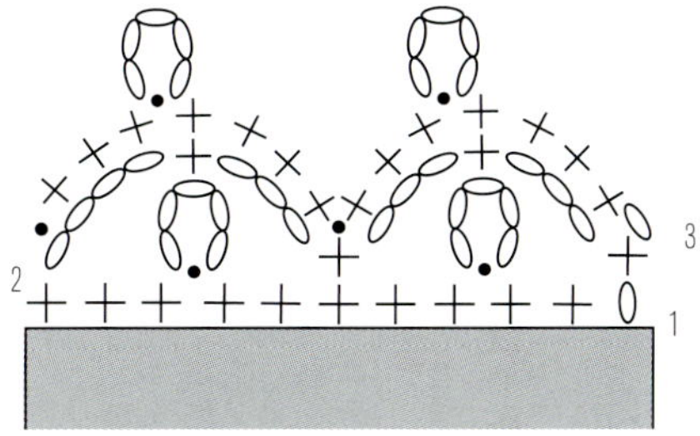

KEY

- Chain
- Slip stitch
- Double

Dangles

Worked lengthways, dangles are an unusual edging to add interest to a plain project.

Begin by working 2 or more rows of dc, ending with a multiple of 3 sts.

Dangle row: 1 ch, skip first dc, 1 dc in next dc, * 6 ch, 3 tr in 3rd ch from hook, 2 ch, 1 ss in ch at base of 3 tr, 1 ss in each of next 3 ch, 1 dc in each of next 3 dc, * repeat from * to * ending 1 dc in last st. Fasten off.

Notes:

- At outward corners, adjust the sts so that a dangle falls on the centre dc of 3 dc worked into the same place.
- This edging may also be worked in rounds.

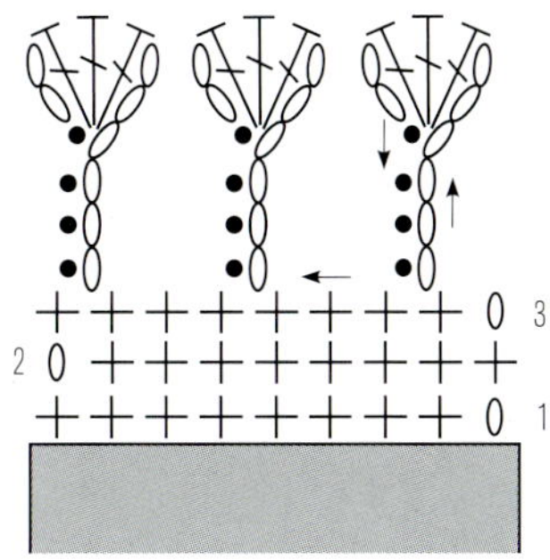

KEY

- Chain
- Slip stitch
- Double
- Treble
- Direction of work

Double shells

Worked sideways, this edging is worked separately and sewn in place (see page 29).

Row 1: 4 ch, 1 tr in first ch made (1 ring made).
Row 2: 3 ch, [2 tr, 2 ch, 3 tr] into ring (1 double shell made), turn.
Row 3: 5 ch *, [1 ss, 3 ch, 1 tr] into 2-ch sp at top of double shell (1 ring made), turn.
Row 4: 3 ch, [2 tr, 2 ch, 3 tr] into ring, 1 tr in 3rd of 5 ch at beg previous row, turn.
Repeat rows 3 and 4 to length required. Fasten off.

Notes:
- At an outward corner, work to length required, ending row 4.

Next row: 3 ch, as row 3 from * to end.
Foll row: As row 4, ending 1 ss in tr at base of 3 ch, turn. Continue in pattern beginning row 3.

KEY
- Chain
- Slip stitch
- Treble
- Direction of work

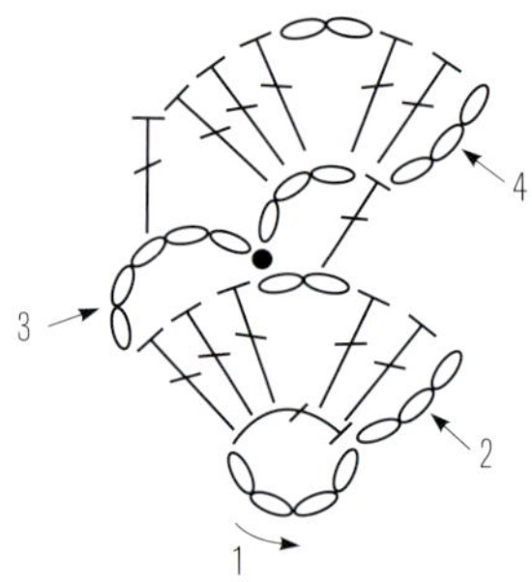

Little flowers

Worked lengthways, this edging may also be worked separately beginning with a foundation chain (multiple of 6 sts, plus 1), then sewn in place (see page 29).

Special abbr: 1 puff: [yrh, insert as given, pull through a loop] 3 times in same place, yrh, pull through first 6 loops on hook, yrh, pull through remaining 2 loops on hook.

Work 1 row of dc, ending with a multiple of 6 sts, plus 1.
Row 2: 1 ch, skip 1 dc, 1 dc in each of next 2 dc, * [1 dc, 4 ch, 1 dc] in next dc, 1 dc in each of 5 dc, * repeat from * to * ending 1 dc in each of last 2 dc, 1 dc in 1 ch.
Row 3: 1 ch, [1 dc, 2 ch, 1 dc] in first dc, * skip 3 dc, [1 puff, 2 ch] twice into 4-ch loop, 1 puff into same place, skip 3 dc, [1 dc, 2 ch, 1 dc] into next dc, * repeat from * to * to end. Fasten off.

Notes:
- At an outward corner, on row 1, adjust the number of dc (see page 28) so that [1 dc, 4 ch, 1 dc] is worked into the centre st of 3 at the corner. On row 2, work [1 puff, 1 ch] 4 times into 4-ch loop at corner, 1 puff in same place.
- To work in rounds, work 1 or more rounds of dc (see page 28), ending with a multiple of 6 sts. Work next round as row 2, ending with 1 ss into first dc of round. Work foll round as row 3, ending skip 3 dc, 1 ss into first dc of round. Fasten off.

KEY
- Chain
- Double
- Puff stitch as described

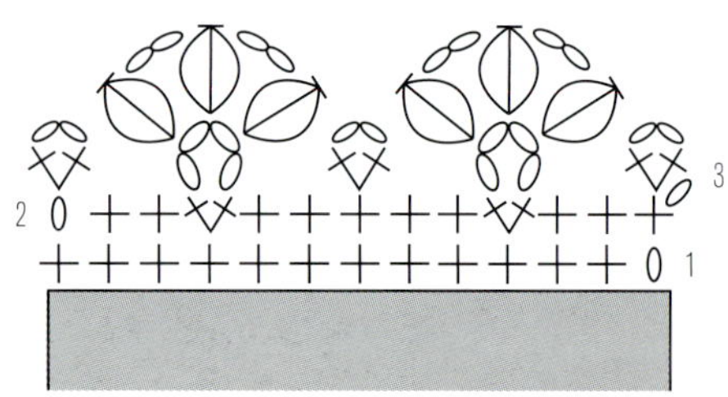

Ribbon edging 1

This edging is worked sideways (see page 29) and then sewn in place.

Work 8 ch.

Row 1: 1 tr in 4th ch from hook, 1 tr in next ch, 2 ch, skip 2 ch, [2 tr, l dtr] in next ch.

Row 2: 5 ch, 1 ss in first of these 5 ch, 1 ss in first dtr, 3 ch, 2 tr tog over 2 tr, 2 ch, skip 2 ch, 1 tr in each of next 2 tr, 1 tr in 3rd of 3 ch.

Row 3: 3 ch, skip first tr, 1 tr in each of next 2 tr, 2 ch, skip 2 ch, [2 tr, 1 dtr] in top of 2 tr tog.

Repeat rows 2 and 3 to length required, ending row 2. Fasten off.

Notes:

- Sew in place and thread with ribbon. At the corners, make tiny pleats in the ribbon on the wrong side of the work, and secure these with needle and thread.
- The number of chains worked may be adjusted to suit ribbons of different widths.

KEY

Chain

Slip stitch

Treble

Double treble

Direction of work

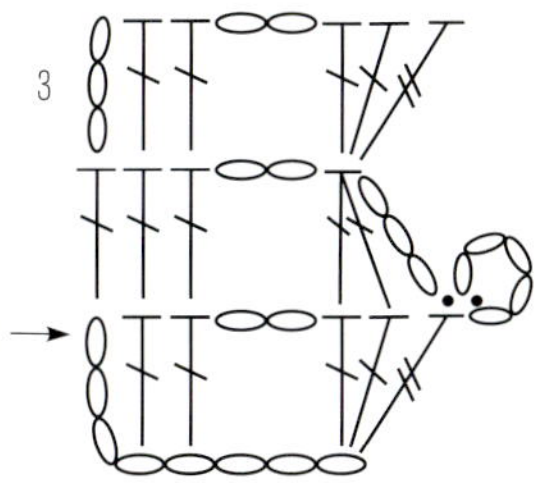

Ribbon edging 2

This ribbon edging is worked lengthways.

Work 2 or more rows of dc, ending with a multiple of 3 sts, plus 1.

Row 3: 5 ch, skip 1st dc, * skip 2 dc, 1 tr in next dc, 2 ch, * repeat from * to *, ending 1 tr in last st.

Row 4: 1 ch, skip first tr, * 3 dc in 2-ch sp, skip 1 tr, * repeat from * to * ending 3 dc in last ch sp, 1 dc in 3rd of 5 ch.

Row 5: 1 ch, skip first dc, 1 dc in each of next 3 dc, * 3 ch, 1 dc in each of 3 dc, * repeat from * to * ending 1 dc in 1 ch. Fasten off.

Notes:

- Thread with ribbon.
- On outward corners, on row 3 work [1 tr, 2 ch] twice, 1 tr all in same place. On row 4 work 3 dc in last ch sp before corner, 2 ch, 3 dc in next ch sp. On row 5 work 1 dc in each of 3 dc before corner, 3 ch, 3 dc in 2-ch sp at corner, 3 ch, 1 dc in each of next 3 dc. Adjust ribbon at corners in same way as for Ribbon edging 1, above.

KEY

Chain

Double

Treble

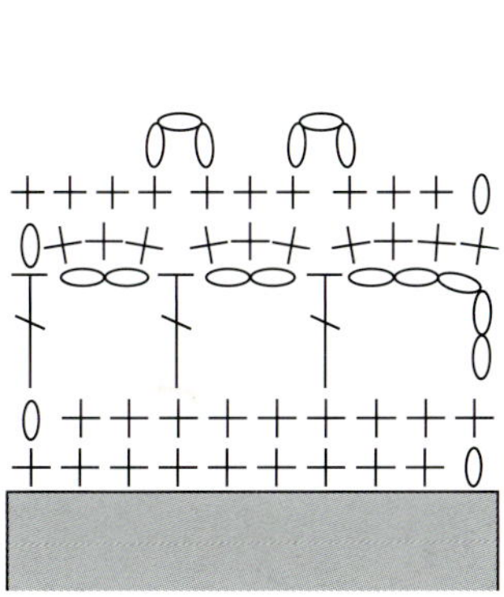

Chain loops

Worked lengthways, this edging is an ideal finish for items such as pillows and throws.

Begin by working 2 or more rows of dc, ending wrong-side row. Any number of sts is suitable.

Fringe row: 1 ch, skip first dc,* [1 dc, 20 ch, 1 ss] in next dc *, repeat from * to * to end. Fasten off.

Notes:

- The length of the fringe is easily adjusted by working more or fewer chains.
- No special treatment is required at corners, provided the preceding rows of dc are worked with increases (or decreases) at corners, as page 27.

KEY

- Chain
- Slip stitch
- Double

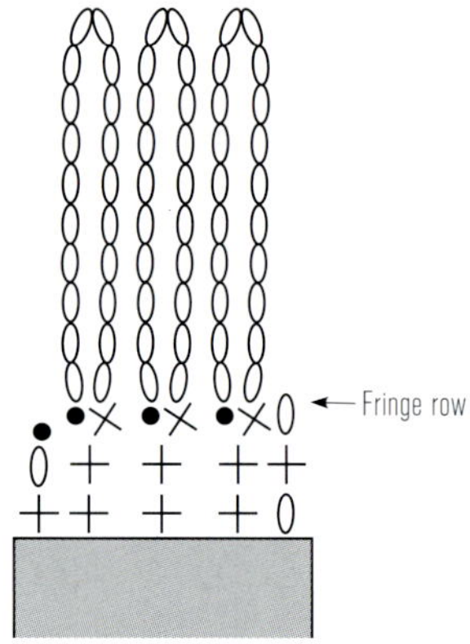

Knotted loops

Worked sideways, this edging is worked separately and sewn in place. It fits easily around corners.

Special abbr: 1 puff: [yrh, insert as given, pull through a loop] 3 times in same place, yrh, pull through first 6 loops on hook, yrh, pull through remaining 2 loops on hook.

Row 1: 13 ch, 1 puff in first ch made. Do not turn the work.

Row 2: 12 ch, 1 puff in top of previous puff (inserting the hook under two threads), do not turn. Repeat row 2 to length required. Fasten off. Sew in place (see page 29).

Note:

The length of the fringe may be adjusted by working more or fewer chains.

KEY

- Chain
- Puff stitch as described
- Do not turn
- Direction of work

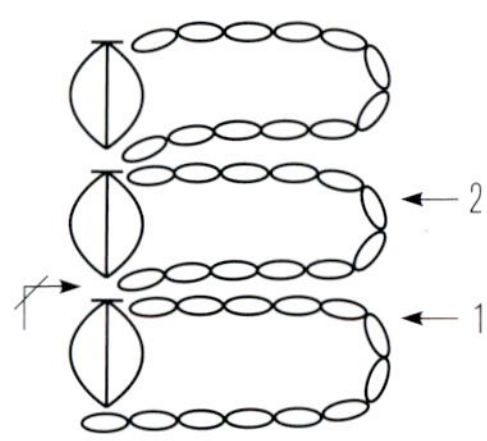

Corkscrew fringe

Worked lengthways, this edging makes a heavy fringe suitable for wraps and throws.

Begin by working 2 or more rows of dc, ending wrong-side row, with a multiple of 3 sts.

Fringe row: 1 ch, skip first dc, 1 dc in next dc, * make 6 ch rather loosely, 3 dc in 2nd ch from hook, 3 dc in each of remaining 4 ch, 1 ss in dc at base of 6 ch (a corkscrew made), 1 dc in each of next 3 dc, * repeat from * to *, ending 1 dc in last st. Fasten off.

Notes:

- At outward corners, work 3 corkscrews in adjacent dc, omitting the dc between them.
- This edging may also be worked in the round.
- Adjust the length of corkscrews by working more than 6 chains.

KEY

- Chain
- Slip stitch
- Double

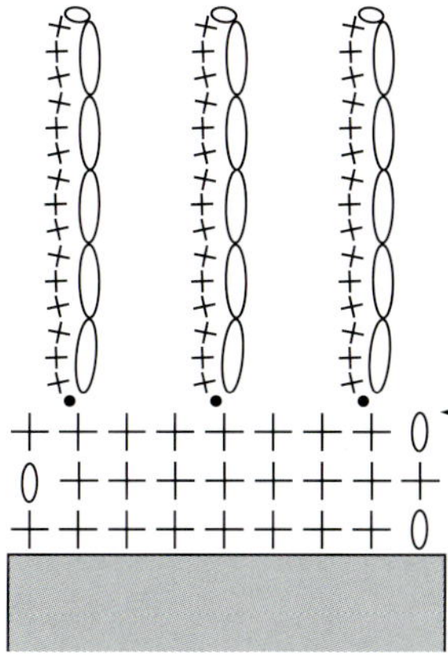

Beaded fringe

This edging is worked lengthways. Thread all the beads required onto the yarn before commencing, as page 56.

Begin by working 2 or more rows of dc, ending with a multiple of 3 sts, plus 2.

Bead row: 1 ch, skip first dc, 1 dc in next dc, * 7 ch, push a bead up the yarn as close to the hook as possible, catch the yarn beyond the bead and work 1 ch, 6 ch, 1 ss in first of 14 ch (a bead loop made), skip 1 dc, 1 dc in each of next 2 dc, * repeat from * to * to end. Fasten off.

Notes:

- At outward corners, work 3 bead loops in adjacent dc, omitting the 2 dc between them.
- May also be worked in the round.

KEY

- Chain
- Slip stitch
- Double
- Bead

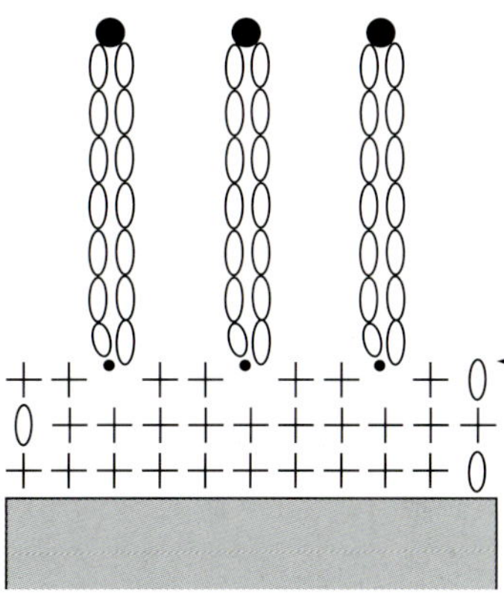

Part 6:

Directory of trims

Pompoms, tassels, spirals, fringes, flowers, stars and hearts: sew-on trims add the personal touch that makes any project unique. Use these trims in any way you choose to decorate your crochet.

Pompoms

Pompoms can be added to the ends of ties and drawstrings on your crocheted garments, or used to embellish the edges and corners of pillows and throws. Or they make a great toy for small children.

Pompom kits

Kits of plastic frames, of various sizes, are available to help you produce traditional fluffy pompoms. Follow the instructions supplied with the kit. For a lovely dense pompom that will resist fraying, wind as much yarn onto the frame(s) as you can before tying the centre as tightly as possible. Leave long tails on the tying strands for attaching the pompom where required. Oddments of different yarns can be used together to produce multicoloured pompoms.

These fluffy pompoms were made with a kit.

Crochet pompoms

Crochet pompoms are fun to make, and more hardwearing than the traditional fluffy kind. The final size will depend on the yarn type and hook used. They are worked in rounds (see pages 118–119), beginning at the centre, and increasing sharply in every stitch so that the frill eventually forms a ball.

The examples shown are made in double crochet for its firmness, but you can experiment with other stitches. By working a different number of dc on round 1, the final fullness of the frilly surface can be adjusted.

Choose a hook size to suit your yarn (see page 8).

Work 6 ch, 1 ss in first ch made to form a ring.

Round 1: 1 ch, 14 dc into ring, 1 ss in 1 ch at beg of round. (= 15 dc)

Round 2: 1 ch, 2 dc in same place as last ss, 3 dc in each dc, ending 1 ss in 1 ch at beg of round. (= 45 dc)

Repeat round 2, 2 more times. Fasten off (leave a long tail for attaching). Roll the pompom between your palms to settle the frills in place.

On the last round, there are 405 dc: 27 dc for each dc of first round. This fullness gives the pompom its shape.

For a looser pompom, begin by working only 10 dc on round 1. The final round will then consist of only 270 dc, making a looser ball. Conversely, working more than 15 dc on round 1 (about 20 dc, perhaps) would make a tighter ball.

Try changing colours as you work the last row, or use a multicoloured yarn.

Tassels, fringes and spirals

Tassels and fringes may be made from cut strands, or they may be crocheted for a firmer result. (Fringes are shown on page 77). Spirals are a fun alternative to tassels.

Cut fringes and tassels

Try using different types of yarn: woollen yarns make soft, light fringes and tassels; cottons, silks and viscose yarns make heavier fringes that drape well.

Simple fringe

1 Cut a rectangle of card, about 2.5cm (1in) wider than the depth of fringe you want. Wind the yarn around the card as many times as required. Cut along one edge to make lots of strands of the same length.

2 Decide on the spacing you want for your fringe, and how many strands to use for each knot. Take two or three strands (three strands are shown above) and fold them in half. Insert a crochet hook through the position required from back through to front and pull the loop of strands through. Then catch the strands and pull them through the loop. Repeat as required. Lay the fringe flat and trim all the strands to the same length.

Beaded fringe

1 Make a simple fringe with extra-long strands. Thread half of the tails from each of two adjacent knots through a large bead and knot with an overhand knot. Use a strip of card to space all the knots equally from the crochet edge.

2 The fringe above was made in green viscose yarn, with large wooden beads. Other arrangements of knots and beads can be found by experiment.

Cut tassel

1 Wind the yarn around a piece of card as for a fringe, left. Thread the tail into a blunt-tipped needle and pass it under the strands at one edge, then back under the last winding as shown, to hold all the strands together. Pull tight.

2 Slip the strands off the card and wind the tail tightly around the tassel, close to the top, several times. Pass the needle back to the centre top and leave the tail uncut for attaching later.

3 Leave the loops uncut, or cut through them and trim them all to the same length.

Crochet tassels

Crochet tassels are more hardwearing than those made from loose strands. These instructions make a tassel approximately 10cm (4in) long in double knitting, or 7.5cm (3in) long in 4-ply, but you can easily vary the length by working more chains to each loop or corkscrew. Vary the fullness by beginning with a different number of chains.

Chain loop tassel

Using hook size to suit yarn, and leaving a long tail, work 19 ch.

Row 1: 1 dc in 2nd ch from hook, 1 dc in each ch to end.

Row 2: 1 ch, skip first dc, 1 dc in each dc, ending 1 dc in 1 ch.

Row 3: 2 ch, skip first dc, * 4 htr tog in next dc, 1 ch, 1 htr in next dc, * repeat from * to *, ending 1 htr in 1 ch.

Row 4: 1 ch, skip [first htr and 1 ch] * 1 dc in top of 4 htr tog, skip 1 htr, 1 dc in ch sp, * repeat from * to * ending 1 dc in 2nd of 2 ch.

Fringe row: 1 ch, [1 dc, 36 ch, 1 ss] in each dc, ending [1 dc, 36 ch, 1 ss] in 1 ch. Fasten off, leaving a long tail.

Tightly roll up the rows of dc and use the starting tail to stitch firmly across the top through all the layers, ending with a stitch at the centre. Use the finishing tail to stitch in and out around the base of the roll and pull up tightly. Secure with a backstitch, then join the side edge of the roll and bring the tail out at centre top. Use the two tails to stitch the tassel where required.

Corkscrew tassel

Using hook size to suit yarn, and leaving a long tail, work 17 ch.

Work rows 1 and 2 as for chain loop tassel. Repeat row 2, four more times.

Row 7: 1 ch, skip first dc, 1 dc in next dc, * 16 ch, 3 dc in 2nd ch from hook, 3 dc in each remaining ch, 1 ss in same place as dc at base of ch [1 corkscrew made], 1 dc in each of next 2 dc, * repeat from * to * ending 1 corkscrew in last st. Fasten off, leaving a long tail.

Roll up and secure in same way as for chain loop tassel.

Crochet spirals

The construction of spirals is similar to that of the corkscrews on the tassel at left, but with several increasing rows. By varying the number of base chains, spirals of different lengths may be made. Use spirals in the same way as tassels to embellish any project.

Basic spiral

Using hook size to suit yarn, make a number of loose chain: the multicolour spiral above begins with 12 ch; the green one with 24 ch.

Row 1: 1 dc in 2nd ch from hook, 2 dc in each ch to end.

Row 2: 1 ch, 1 dc in first dc, 2 dc in each dc to end.

Repeat row 2, two or more times. Fasten off, leaving a long tail for attachment.

Stroke the spiral between your fingers to even out the coils.

Spirals may be made any length required. They look very effective in stripes – here, the two ends of an 20cm (8in) spiral are joined to make a bracelet.

Flowers

Use crochet flowers to add the finishing touch to accessories such as hats and purses, or stitch one to a brooch pin to wear on any garment.

Four, five or six-petal flower

The chart shows the five-petal version of this flower. The four-petal and six-petal versions are constructed in a similar way. Instructions are given below for four [five, six] petals, using two colours, A and B.

Using colour A, make 5[7, 9] ch, 1 ss in first ch made to close the ring.

Round 1: 1 ch, 11[14, 17] dc into ring, 1 ss into 1 ch at beginning of round. Fasten off A.

Round 2: Join colour B to any dc, 4 ch, * 4 dtr tog, inserting hook twice into next dc, and twice into foll dc, 3 ch, 1 dc in next dc, 3 ch, * repeat from * to * 2[3, 4] more times, 4 dtr tog as before, 3 ch, 1 ss in first ch of round. Fasten off B.

KEY

- Chain
- Slip stitch
- Double
- Join in
- Fasten off
- Double treble

Waterlily

For the small version, work rounds 1 and 2 only, then fasten off with 1 ss in first dc of round 2.

For the medium version, work rounds 1–4, then fasten off with 1 ss in first dc of round 4.

For the large version, work all 6 rounds.

Instructions are given for using two colours, A and B.

Using colour A, make 8 ch, 1 ss in first ch made to close the ring.

Round 1: 6 ch, [1 tr into ring, 3 ch] 7 times, 1 ss in 3rd of 6 ch at beg of round. Fasten off A.

Round 2: Join colour B to any 3-ch sp, [1 dc, 2 ch, 3 tr, 2 ch, 1 dc] into same sp, * 1 dc, 2 ch, 3 tr, 2 ch, 1 dc] into next 3-ch sp *, repeat from * to * 6 more times, do not join. (8 petals made.)

Round 3: Working behind petals of previous round, * 5 ch, miss 1 petal, 1 dc in top of next tr of round 1 *, repeat from * to * 7 more times, do not join. (8 loops made.)

Round 4: * [1 dc, 2 ch, 5 tr, 2 ch, 1 dc] into next 5-ch loop *, repeat from * to * 7 more times, do not join.
(8 petals made.)

Round 5: Working behind petals of previous round, * 7 ch, miss 1 petal, 1 dc in next dc of round 3 *, repeat from * to * 7 more times, do not join.
(8 loops made.)

Round 6: * [1 dc, 2 ch, 7 tr, 2 ch, 1 dc] into next 7-ch loop *, repeat from * to * 7 more times, 1 ss in first dc of round. Fasten off B.

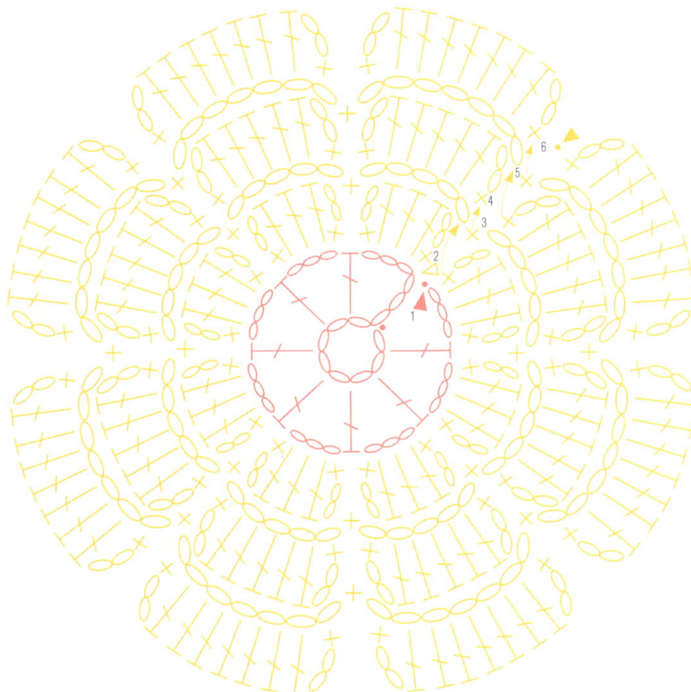

KEY

- Chain
- Double
- Treble
- Slip stitch
- Fasten off
- Join in
- Begin next row without joining

Spiral flower

Make 33 ch.

Beginning in 2nd ch from hook, 2 htr in each of 10 ch, 2 tr in each of 10 ch, 2 dtr in each of 10 ch, 2 tr in each of 2 ch, 2 htr in last ch. Fasten off.

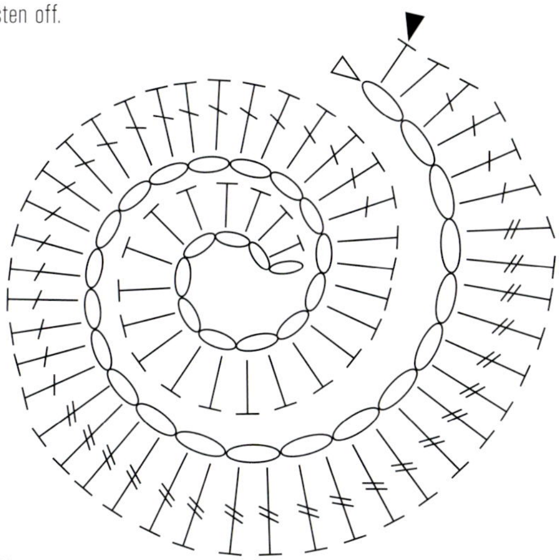

KEY

- Chain
- Half-treble
- Treble
- Double treble
- Begin
- Fasten off

Aster

Instruction below use two colours, A and B.

Using A, make 4 ch, 1 ss in first ch made to close the ring.

Round 1: 1 ch, 11 dc into ring, change to colour B, 1 ss in first ch of round. Do not cut A.

Round 2: Using B, [1 dc, 4 ch, 1 dc] in front loop of first ch and front loop of each dc of previous round, 1 ss in first dc of round. Fasten off B. (12 petals made.)

Round 3: Using A, [1 ss, 7 ch, 1 dc] in back loop of first ch, [1 dc, 7 ch, 1 dc] in back loop of each dc of round 1, 1 ss in first ss of round. Fasten off. (12 more petals made.)

You can vary the lengths of the petals by working more or fewer chains for each petal.

KEY

- Chain
- Slip stitch
- Double
- Join in
- Fasten off
- Double in front loop
- Double in back loop

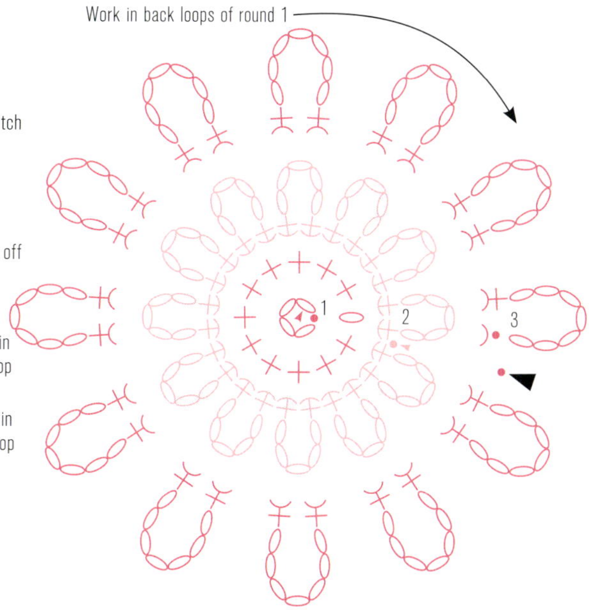

Chrysanthemum

Make 5 ch, 1 ss in 3rd ch from hook, 2 ch, 1 dc in first ch made, do not turn.

[5 ch, 1 ss in 3rd ch from hook, 2 ch, 1 dc in last dc made, do not turn] 8 times.

[7 ch, 1 ss in 3rd ch from hook, 4 ch, 1 dc in last dc made, do not turn] 9 times.

[9 ch, 1 ss in 3rd ch from hook, 6 ch, 1 dc in last dc made, do not turn] 9 times.

Fasten off leaving a long tail. Arrange the petals in a spiral and use the long tail to stitch across the back to hold the spiral in place.

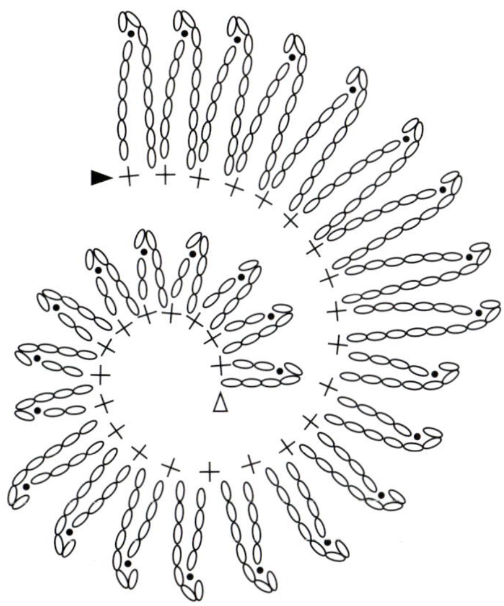

KEY

- Chain
- Slip stitch
- Double
- Begin
- Fasten off

Stars and hearts

Sew stars or hearts to pillows or blankets, or hang them as decorations for parties or celebrations.

Six-pointed star

Note: Instructions for working extended dc (abbreviation: xdc) appear on page 117.

Using colour A (peach), begin with 2 ch.

Row 1: 1 dc in 2nd ch from hook.

Row 2: 1 ch, 2 dc in dc.

Row 3: 1 ch, 2 dc in first dc, 1 dc in dc.

Row 4: 1 ch, 2 dc in first dc, 1 dc in each of 2 dc. 4 dc.

Row 5: 5 ch, 2 dc tog in 2nd and 3rd chs from hook, 1 dc in each of 2 ch, 1 dc in each of 4 dc, 4 xdc. 11 sts.

Row 6: 1 ch, 2 dc tog over first and 2nd xdc, 1 dc in each st to end. 10 sts.

Repeat row 6, twice more. 8 sts.

Row 9: 1 ch, 2 dc in first dc, 1 dc in each dc to end. 9 sts.

Repeat row 9, 3 more times. 12 sts.

Row 13: 1 ch, 1 ss in each of first 5 dc, 1 ch, 1 dc in same dc as last ss, 1 dc in each of next 3 dc, turn leaving last 4 dc unworked.

Row 14: 1 ch, 2 dc tog over first and second dc, 1 dc in each of 2 dc.

Row 15: 1 ch, 2 dc tog over first and second dc, 1 dc in last dc.

Row 16: 1 ch, 2 dc tog over remaining 2 sts. Fasten off.

Last round: (not shown on chart) Join B to any point. 4 ch, 1 dc in same place as base of 4 ch, * 2 dc down side edge of point, 2 dc tog at inner corner, 2 dc up side edge of next point, [1 dc, 3 ch, 1 dc] at outer point, * repeat from * to * ending last repeat with 1 ss into 1st of 4 ch at beg of round. Fasten off.

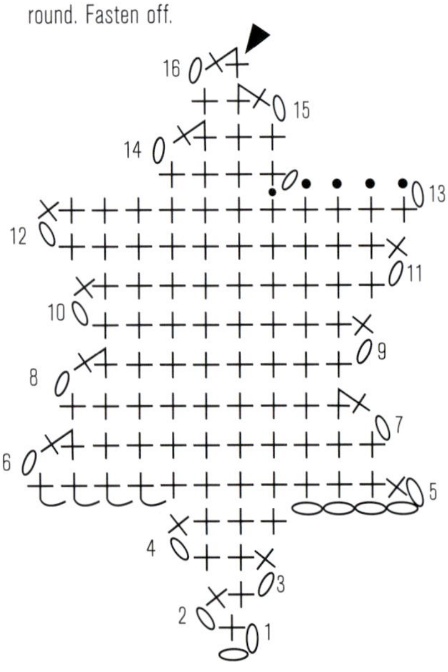

KEY

- Chain
- Double
- Slip stitch
- Extended double
- Fasten off
- 2 double crochet together

Little five-pointed star

Begin with 4 ch, join into a ring with 1 ss in first ch made.

Round 1: 3 ch, 14 tr into centre of ring, 1 ss in 3rd of 3 ch at beg of round.

Round 2: * 3 ch, 2 dtr tog over next 2 tr, 3 ch, 1 ss through top front loops of 2 dtr tog below (a picot made), 3 ch, 1 ss in next tr, * repeat from * to *, working last ss in same place as base of 3 ch at beg of round. Fasten off.

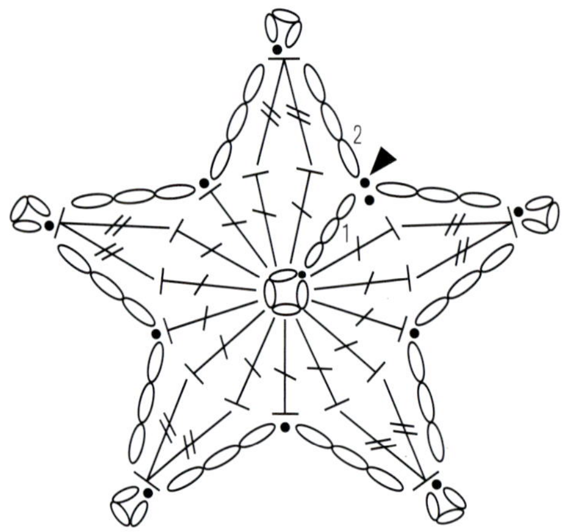

KEY

- Chain
- Slip stitch
- Treble
- Double treble
- Fasten off

Large five-pointed star

Using A, make 4 ch and join into a ring with 1 ss into first ch made.
Round 1: 3 ch, 14 tr into centre of ring, 1 ss in 3rd of 3 ch at beg of round.
Round 2: 3 ch, [2 tr in next tr, 2 htr in next tr, 2 tr in next tr] 5 times, ending 1 tr in same place as base of 3 ch, 1 ss in 3rd of 3 ch at beg of round. 30 sts.

First point

Row 1: 3 ch, skip first tr, 1 tr in next tr, 2 tr tog over 2 htr, 1 tr in each of next 2 tr, turn.
Row 2: 2 ch, skip first tr, 4 tr tog over next 3 sts and 3rd of 3 ch, 1 ch. Fasten off.

Second point

With right side facing, rejoin A to next unworked tr of round 2. Work as for first point.
Work 3 more points in the same way.
Last round: (not shown on chart) Join B to any point. 3 ch, 1 dc in same place as base of ch, * 4 dc down side edge of point, 3 dc tog at inner corner, 4 dc up side edge of next point, [1 dc, 2 ch, 1 dc] at outer point, * repeat * to *, ending last repeat with 1 ss into 1st of 3 ch at beg of round. Fasten off.

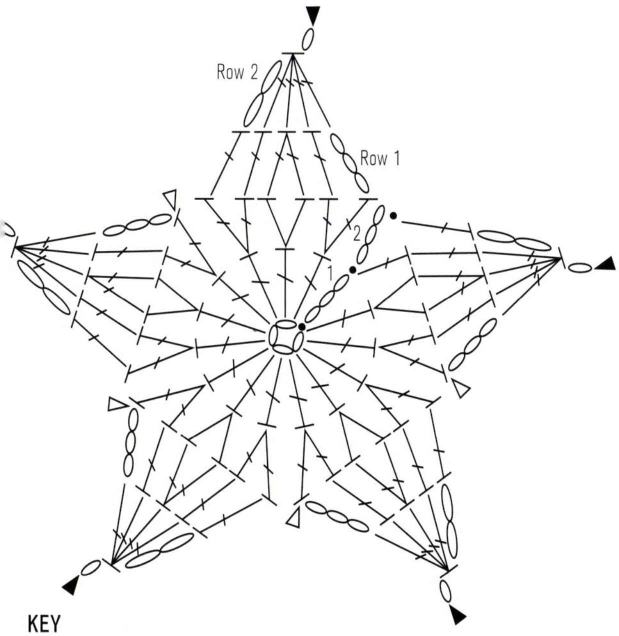

KEY

- Chain
- Slip stitch
- Half-treble
- Treble
- Join in
- Fasten off

Large heart

Begin with 10 ch.
Round 1: 1 dc in 2nd ch from hook, 1 dc in each of next 2 ch, 2 dc tog over next and alt ch, 1 dc in each of next 2 ch, 5 dc in first ch made. Work along lower loops of ch: 1 dc in each of next 3 loops, [1 dc, 2 ch, 1 dc] in next loop, 1 dc in each of next 3 loops, 4 dc in next loop, 1 ss in first dc of round.
Round 2: 1 ch, 1 dc in each of 2 dc, 2 dc tog over next and alt st (skipping top of 2 dc tog), 1 dc in each of 3 dc, 3 dc in next dc, 1 dc in each of 6 dc, [1 dc, 2 ch, 1 dc] in 2-ch sp, 1 dc in each of 6 dc, 3 dc in next dc, 1 dc in next dc, 1 ss in first dc of round, fasten off.
Round 3: Join another colour to same place. 1 ch, 1 dc in next dc, 3 dc tog over next 3 sts, 1 dc in each of 2 dc, 2 dc in each of next 3 dc, 1 dc in each of 7 dc, [1 dc, 2 ch, 1 dc] in 2-ch sp, 1 dc in each of 7 dc, 2 dc in each of next 3 dc, 1 dc in next dc, 1 ss in first dc of round, fasten off.

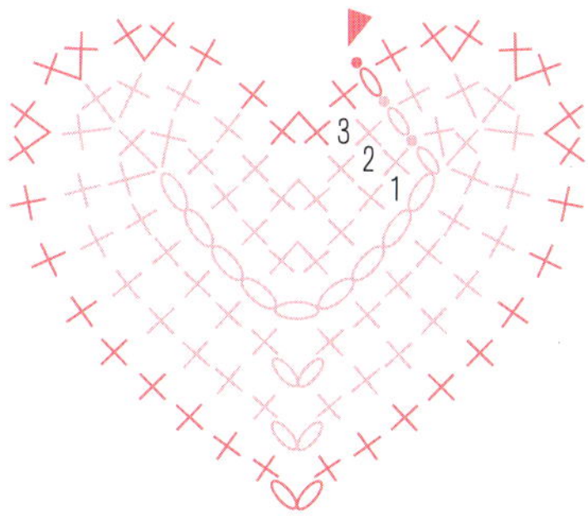

KEY

- Chain
- Slip stitch
- Double
- Fasten off
- 2 double crochet together

Small hearts

Work rounds 1 and 2 as for large heart above, omitting round 3. Fasten off.
For a tiny heart as shown, work in fine yarn with a smaller hook than the recommended size, e.g. 3-ply yarn with a size 1.5–2mm hook.

Part 7:

Adaptable Projects

Each project in this section has been designed to be adapted in various ways, using techniques described elsewhere in this book. Follow the instructions, or invent your own version – from a simple scarf to a lacy jacket or a felted rug, you can add your own choice of stitch, edging, or trim to make a one-off original design. All abbreviations are listed on page 123.

Daisy stitch scarf

The fascinating stitch pattern used for this scarf is simple to work once you've tried it, and ideal for a scarf because it looks the same on both sides.

Scarf

Using hook size 5.5mm make 41 ch (a multiple of 3 ch, plus 5).

Daisy Stitch

Row 1: 3 tr tog, inserting hook in [3rd, 5th, and 8th ch from hook], * 2 ch, 3 tr tog, inserting hook in [stitch closing previous group, same ch as last insertion of previous group, and following 3rd ch], * repeat from * to * to end. 12 daisy clusters made.

Row 2: 5 ch, 3 tr tog, inserting hook in [3rd ch from hook, stitch closing last group of previous row, and stitch closing next group, * 2 ch, 3 tr tog inserting hook in [stitch closing previous group of this row, same place as last insertion of previous group and stitch closing next group] * repeat from * to * making last insertion of last group into 3rd of 5 ch at beginning of previous row.

Repeat row 2 to length 120cm (48in) or as required. Fasten off.

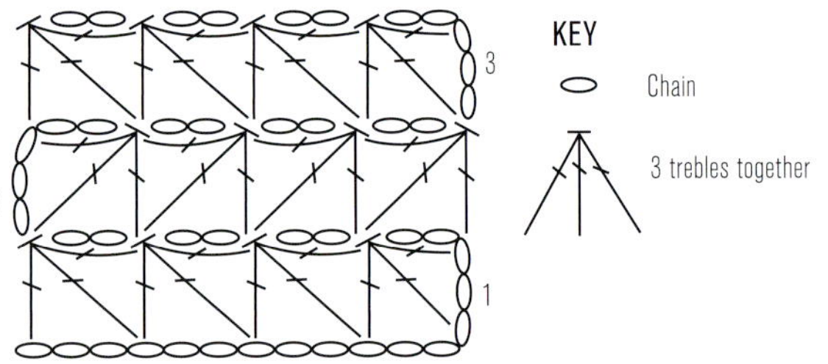

To finish

Add a beaded fringe, as page 80, cutting strands to 25cm (10in) to make a generous length of fringe.

Size

Adult size: Width approx. 20cm (8in), length 120cm (48in) or as required.

Materials

- Aran weight 100% wool (approx. 76m per 50g / 48 yards per oz): 225g
- Approx. 24 large beads
- Hook size 5.5mm, or size to obtain correct tension
- Yarn needle

Tension

- 6 patterns and 7 rows to 10cm (4in) measured over Daisy Stitch, as left. Tension is not crucial if a different finished width is acceptable, but if your tension is incorrect, extra yarn may be required (see page 6).

Be your own designer

A scarf is a great project if you want to try out an unusual stitch or new technique. Make a scarf in any suitable stitch and yarn, as follows:

- Choose a suitable stitch: bear in mind that when worn, both sides of a scarf will be visible.
- Choose a soft, smooth yarn that will be comfortable to wear around the neck.
- Choose a hook size to suit your yarn (see page 8).
- Make a tension sample (see page 6) and count your tension.
- Suppose your tension is 20 stitches to 10cm (4in). For a width of 20cm (8in) you would need 2 x 20 = 40 stitches.
- For a more complex pattern, the width is counted in pattern repeats: suppose you have 5 ½ pattern repeats to 10cm (4in). For a width of 20cm (8in) you would need 2 x 5 ½ = 11 pattern repeats. (If necessary, adjust the width slightly to suit a whole number of pattern repeats.)

The fancy yarn used for this sample suits a simple stitch such as this **Large Offset Mesh**:

Begin with an odd number of ch, plus 3:

Row 1: 1 tr in 4th ch from hook, * 1 ch, skip 1 ch, 1 tr in next ch, * repeat from * to * to end.

Row 2: 3 ch, skip 1st tr, * 1 tr in 1 ch sp, 1 ch, skip 1 tr, * repeat from * to *, working last tr in 3rd of 3 ch. Repeat Row 2.

This sample is finished with an edging of Dangles (see page 73).

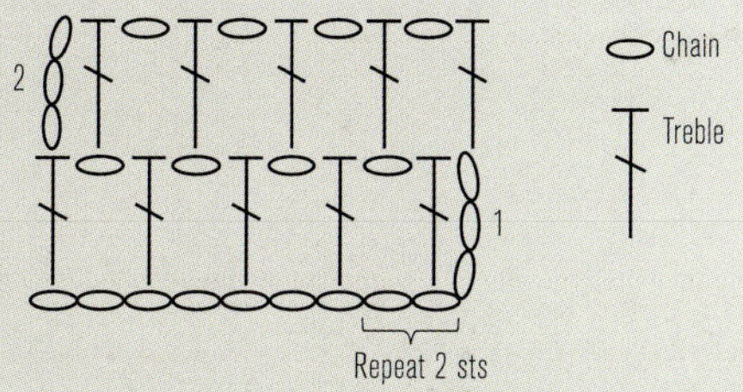

Woven tote bag

This useful tote bag is both pretty and practical. The woven crochet makes a firm fabric, strong enough to carry books or groceries. Make one in your favourite colours, or adapt the design as suggested opposite.

Finished size

30.5 x 23cm (12 x 9in) excluding handles

Materials

- Lightweight double knitting 100% cotton yarn (approx. 105m per 50g / 64 yards per oz):

Colour A (primrose): 250g
Colour B (pink): 25g
Colour C (pale blue): 25g

- Hook size G (4mm)
- Yarn needle

Tension

- 12 patterns and 11 rows to 10cm (4in) measured over Mesh Pattern (as worked in the main panel), using size 4mm hook. Tension is not crucial provided a change in size is acceptable. However, if your tension is too loose, the bag may stretch out of shape, and extra yarn could be required.

Abbreviations

- See page 123

Main panel

Using size 4mm hook and col. A, make 75 ch.

Row 1: 1 tr in 4th ch from hook, 1 tr in next ch, * 1 ch, skip 1 ch, 1 tr in next ch, * repeat from * to * 35 times, 1 tr in last ch, turn: 35 mesh holes.

Row 2: 3 ch, skip first tr, 1 tr in next tr, * 1 ch, skip 1 ch, 1 tr in next tr, * repeat from * to * 35 times, 1 tr in 3rd of 3 ch at beg previous row, turn.

Repeat row 2, 20 more times, placing a stitch marker at each end of the last row.

Repeat row 2, 9 more times, placing a stitch marker at each end of last row.

Repeat row 2, 22 more times. 53 rows in all. Fasten off.

Work the weaving

Cut 44 x 76cm (30in) lengths of col. B and 26 x 76cm (30in) lengths of col. C. Take two lengths of col. B and tie an overhand knot about 5cm (2in) from one end. Thread the other ends into the tapestry needle and weave the right hand column of vertical mesh holes by the method shown on

page 54. Leave the tails free at the top of the column. Alternating the 'overs' and 'unders' of each column, weave the next 7 columns with col. B, then [1 column with col. C, 1 column with col. B] 3 times, 7 columns with col. C, [1 column with col. B, 1 column with col. C] 3 times, and the remaining 8 columns with col. B.
When the weaving is complete, gently stretch the panel lengthways to settle the woven strands in place. Then pass each free tail separately around the top bar, and knot them in pairs with an overhand knot. Trim all the tails to 2.5cm (1in) below the knots.

Side panel (make 2)

Using size 4mm hook and col. A, make 21 ch.
Row 1: 1 tr in 4th ch from hook, 1 tr in each ch to end, turn. 19 tr.
Row 2: 3 ch, skip first tr, 1 tr in each tr, ending 1 tr in 3rd of 3 ch, turn.
Repeat row 2, 20 more times. 22 rows in all. Fasten off.

Assemble panels

With right sides of panels facing, pin or tack one side panel to the main panel, matching the lower corners to the marked rows, and matching the top corners. Begin at top right corner of side panel, with right side of main panel towards you. Using size 4mm hook and col. A, work a double crochet seam all around to top left corner of side panel, working 2 dc in side edge of every row of both thicknesses together. Fasten off. Join the second side panel in place in the same way.

Top edge

With right side of bag facing, join col. A to top of one side seam at right corner of main panel.
Round 1: Using size 4mm hook, work along top edge of main panel: 1 ch, 1 dc in next tr, * 1 dc in 1 ch sp to right of woven thread, 1 dc in same ch sp to left of woven thread, skip 1 tr, * repeat from * to * ending 1 dc in last tr. Work along top of side panel, working 1 dc in each tr. Work along top edges of other side of main panel, and second side panel, in the same way, ending 1 ss into 1 ch at beg of round. Do not turn.
Round 2: 1 ch, 1 dc in each dc, ending 1 ss into 1 ch at beg of round. Do not turn. Repeat round 2, 3 more times. 5 rounds made. Fasten off.

Handles (make 2)

With right side of bag facing, using size 4mm hook, join col. A to top edge, directly above the first line woven in col. C (counting from the right).
Row 1: 1 ch, 1 dc in same place, 1 dc in each of next 9 dc, turn. 10 sts.
Row 2: 1 ch, 1 dc in each dc to end.
Repeat row 2 until handle measures 28cm (11in), ending with a wrong side row. Without twisting, match the last handle row to the top edge of the bag in a position to match the beginning of the handle. Working from the inside of the bag, work 1 row dc through both thicknesses and fasten off. Work the second handle in the same way.

Borders

Join col. A to one top corner of the bag. Work 1 ch, then work 1 round of ss, all around the top edge and outer edges of handles, working 1 ss in each st and in side edge of each row, with 3 ss together at each handle corner, and ending 1 ss into first ss of round. Fasten off.
Work all around inside edge of each handle in the same way.

To finish

Run in any remaining yarn tails. If required, block the tote bag as shown on page 24, stuff it with bubble wrap, and leave to dry.

Be your own designer

1. Change the yarn: use a finer yarn, such as 4-ply, and a suitable hook to make a correspondingly smaller bag or purse. Use a heavier yarn, such as aran or worsted weight, with a suitable hook, to make a larger tote.

2. Change the weaving pattern: work the mesh in any way you choose (see page 54 for more ideas).

3. Change the look: the mesh panel may be decorated with surface crochet instead of weaving (see page 55). Work all the panels in tr (as given for the side panels), then decorate with your own choice of embellishments (see pages 82–85).

2 Surface crochet (see page 55)

3 Spiral flower (see page 83)

Beaded purse

Make this beaded purse in colours to suit a special dress, or as gift for a friend. Adapt the design with your own choice of beads or other trimmings.

Size

Approx. 17.5 x 20cm (7 x 8in)

Materials

- Lightweight double knitting 100% cotton yarn (approx. 120m per 50g / 144 yards): approx. 100g
- 84 pearly beads, to fit easily onto yarn
- 1 button, or small plastic ring plus 1 more bead
- Hook size 3.5mm
- Yarn needle

Tension

- First 2 rounds of beaded square should measure approx. 5 x 5cm (2 x 2in), but tension is not crucial provided a change in size is acceptable. Do not work loosely: a firm fabric works best for this design.

Abbreviations

See page 123

Special abbreviation:

btr = treble crochet stitch with a bead, as shown on page 56.

Flap and back

Begin with the beaded square, which forms the flap and top of the purse:

Thread 84 beads onto yarn (see page 56). The square is worked in rounds, beginning at the centre (see page 120), and the beads will appear on the back of the square, not on the side facing as you work:

Work 4 ch, join into a ring with 1 ss in first ch made.

Round 1: 6 ch, * 3 tr into ring, 3 ch, * repeat from * to * twice more, 2 tr into ring, ss in 3rd of 6 ch at beginning of round. 3 tr on each side of square.

Round 2: Ss into each of next 2 ch, 6 ch, [1 tr, 1 btr] in same 3-ch sp, * tr in next tr, btr in foll tr, tr in foll tr, [1 btr, 1 tr, 3 ch, 1 tr, 1 btr] in next 3-ch sp, * repeat from * to * twice more, tr in next tr, btr in foll tr, tr in next tr, 1 btr in next ch sp, ss in 3rd of 6 ch. 7 tr on

The beaded purse is shown here in cream yarn. The smaller beige purse is the version described in the box, opposite.

each side of square. (Square should measure approx. 5 x 5cm / 2 x 2in).

Round 3: Ss into each of next 2 ch, 6 ch, 2 tr in same 3-ch sp, * 1 tr in each btr and tr to next ch sp, [2 tr, 3 ch, 2 tr] in 3-ch sp, * repeat from * to * twice more, 1 tr in each btr and tr to next ch sp, 1 tr in this ch sp, ss in 3rd of 6 ch. 11 tr on each side of square.

Round 4: Ss into each of next 2 ch, 6 ch, [1 tr, 1 btr] in same 3-ch sp, * [tr in next tr, btr in foll tr,] 5 times, tr in foll tr, [1 btr, 1 tr, 3 ch, 1 tr, 1 btr] in next 3-ch sp, * repeat from * to * twice more, [tr in next tr, btr in foll tr] 5 times, tr in next tr, 1 btr in next ch sp, ss in 3rd of 6 ch. 15 tr on each side of square.

Round 5: As round 3. 19 tr on each side of square.

Round 6: Ss into each of next 2 ch, 6 ch, [1 tr, 1 btr] in same 3-ch sp, * [tr in next tr, btr in foll tr] 9 times, tr in foll tr, [1 btr, 1 tr, 3 ch, 1 tr, 1 btr] in next 3-ch sp, * repeat from * to * twice more, [tr in next tr, btr in foll tr] 9 times, tr in next tr, 1 btr in next ch sp, ss in 3rd of 6 ch. 23 tr on each side of square.

Now continue in rows: Turn the work, so the beaded side is facing you.

Back row 1 (right side row): (work in back loops of tr of previous row): 2 ch, skip first st, 2 tr tog over next 2 sts, 1 tr in each of next 20 sts to ch sp, [2 tr, 3 ch, 2 tr] in 3-ch sp, 1 tr in each of next 20 sts, 3 tr tog over next 3 sts, turn. Continue on these sts only:

Back row 2: (work in front loops of tr of previous row): 2 ch, skip top of 3 tr tog, 2 tr tog over next 2 tr, 1 tr in each of 20 tr, [2 tr, 3 ch, 2 tr] in 3-ch sp, 1 tr in each of 20 tr, 3 tr tog over last 2 tr and top of 2 tr tog, turn.

Back row 3: as row 2, but work in back loops of tr of previous row.

Repeat Back rows 2 and 3, twice more, and Back row 2 once again. 8 rows in all. Fasten off.

Edging

With right side of piece facing, rejoin yarn to 3-ch sp at top point of flap.

Round 1: 1 ch, 1 dc in same ch sp, 1 dc in each st to next ch sp, 2 dc in 3-ch sp, 19 dc down side edge of rows to next corner (placing a marker on 3rd dc of 19), 2 dc in same place at corner, 1 dc in each st to next ch sp, 3 dc in 3-ch sp, 1 dc in each st to next corner, 2 dc in same place, 19 dc up side edge of rows to next corner (placing a marker on 17th dc of 19), 2 dc in 3-ch sp, 1 dc in each st to last ch sp, 1 dc in 3-ch sp, 1 ss in 1 ch at beginning of round. Fasten off.

Purse flap and back

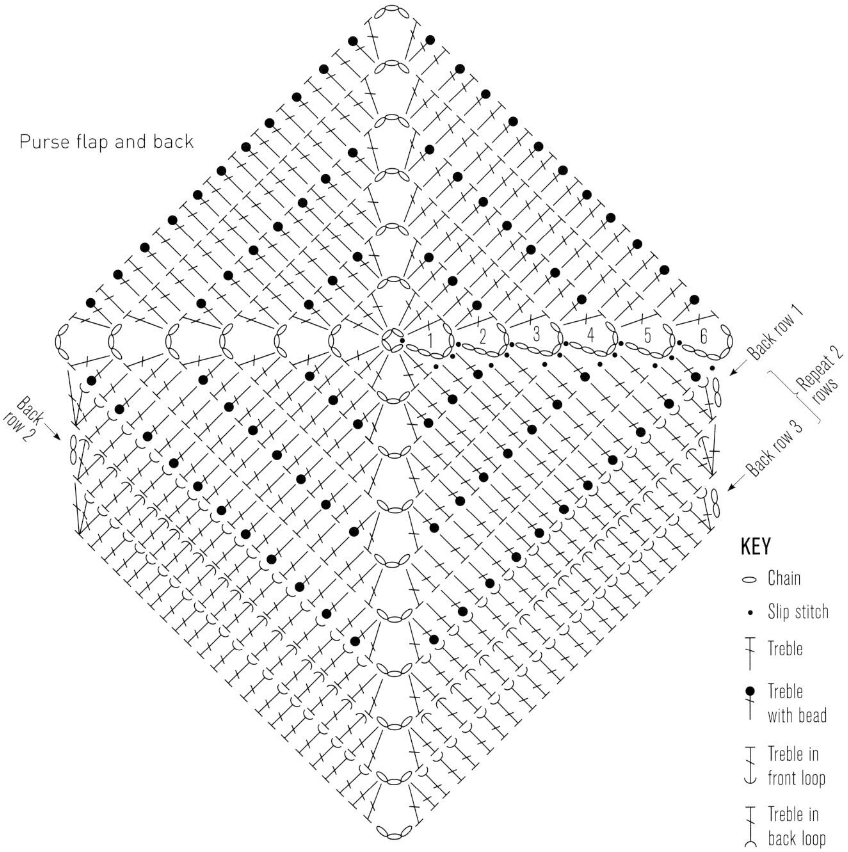

Be your own designer

The size of the purse may be varied by changing the yarn weight and corresponding hook size (choose a hook one size smaller than recommended for your yarn).

The smaller purse in the photograph (opposite) was made in 4-ply cotton yarn, using a size 2.5mm hook, with a contrasting pearlised yarn for the edgings and flower trim (see Aster, page 83). The beads were omitted, and instead of a button, a press fastener was sewn beneath the tip of the flap. The shorter handle is approx. 30cm (12in) long, made in the same way as for the handle of the cream purse, but made wider by adding four more rows of double crochet.

Front

This piece begins with a triangle, worked in rows: Work 4 ch and join into a ring with 1 ss in first ch made.

Front row 1: 5 ch, [3 tr, 3 ch, 3 tr] into ring, 1 ch, 1 dtr into ring, turn.

Front row 2: (work in back loops of tr of previous row): 5 ch, 2 tr in first ch sp, 1 tr in each tr to next ch sp, [2 tr, 3 ch, 2 tr] in 3-ch sp, 1 tr in each tr to last ch sp, 2 tr under 5 ch, 1 ch, 1 dtr in 3rd of 5ch.

Front row 3: as row 2, but work in front loops of tr of previous row.

Repeat Front rows 2 and 3 once more.

Front row 6: work as row 2, but begin 4 ch, and end 2 tr under 5 ch, 1 ch, 1 dtr in 3rd of 5 ch. 6 rows in all. 23 tr on each of two sides of triangle, between ch sps.

Front row 7: (work in front loops of tr of previous row): 1 ss in ch, 1 ss in next tr, 2 ch, 2 tr tog over next 2 tr, 1 tr in each of 20 tr, [2 tr, 3 ch, 2 tr] in 3-ch sp, 1 tr in each of 20 tr, 3 tr tog over last 3 tr.

Front row 8: (work in back loops of tr of previous row): 2 ch, skip top of 3 tr tog, 2 tr tog over next 2 tr, 1 tr in each of 20 tr, [2 tr, 3 ch, 2 tr] in 3-ch sp, 1 tr in each of 20 tr, 3 tr tog over last 2 tr and top of 2 tr tog, turn.

Front row 9: as Front row 8, but work in front loops of tr of previous row.

Repeat Front rows 8 and 9, twice more. 7 rows from triangle – 1 row less than Back. Fasten off.

Edging

With right side facing, rejoin yarn to ch sp at top left of straight edge (end of Front row 6):

Round 1: 1 ch, 1 dc in same place, 16 dc down side edge of rows to next corner, 2 dc in same place at corner, 1 dc in each st to next ch sp, 3 dc in 3-ch sp, 1 dc in each st to next corner, 2 dc in same place, 16 dc up side edge of rows to next corner, 3 dc in same place at corner, work across top edge: 3 dc in side edge of each row and 1 dc in ring at center, ending 1 dc at top left corner, ss in 1 ch at beg of round. Do not fasten off.

Joining round: Place Back and Front with wrong sides together, with Front facing you, 1 ch, work through both layers together: 1 dc in next dc together with 3rd (marked) dc of Back, 1 dc in each pair of dc all around to top right corner of Front, ending in second marked dc of Back. The corners should match exactly. Fasten off.

Flap edging

With right side of Flap facing, join yarn at right corner of beaded square, in side edge of first dc of joining round.

1 ch, 1 dc in each dc to corner, make button loop to fit button at corner (see page 39), 1 dc in each dc along second edge, ending 1 ss in side edge of last dc of joining round. Fasten off.

Sew on button to match button loop: the cream purse in the photograph is finished with a ring button, as shown on page 43, with an extra bead sewn at the centre.

Handle

Work 200 ch (for a handle approx. 90cm [36in] long), or length required.

Row 1: Turn the chain, skip first ch, 1 dc in back loop of each ch to end (see page 13).

Sew the ends of the handles inside the top corners of the purse.

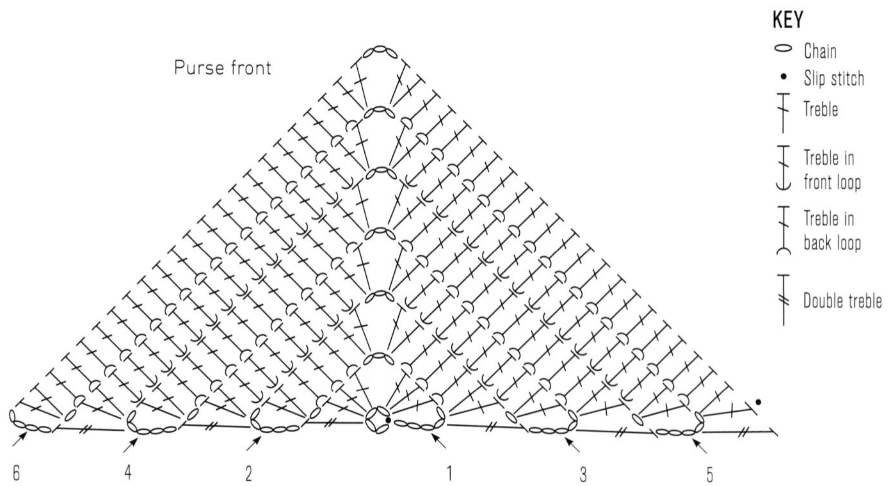

Child's sweater

This basic sweater pattern, worked mainly in treble crochet, can be adapted in a number of ways. Any yarn of suitable weight may be used. Make it in stripes, add trims and different edgings, or even a picture motif (see pages 94–95).

Back

Using hook size E (3.5mm), make 54[60, 66, 72, 78] ch.

Row 1: 1 tr in 4th ch from hook, 1 tr in each ch to end. 52[58, 64, 70, 76] tr.

Row 2: 3 ch, skip first tr, 1 tr in each tr, ending 1 tr in 3rd of 3 ch.

Repeat row 2 until Back measures 17[19, 22, 24.5, 26.5]cm / 6 ¾[7 ½, 8 ½, 9 ½, 10 ¼]in, ending wrong-side row.

Shape raglan armholes

Dec row 1: Skipping first st, 1 ss in each of next 5 tr, 2 ch, 1 tr in each tr to last 7 sts, 2 tr tog, turn. 40[46, 52, 58, 64] sts. (At each end of the row, 5 sts have been skipped, and 1 st decreased.)

Dec row 2: 3 ch, skip 2 tr tog, 1 tr in each tr ending 1 tr in last tr. (1 row worked without shaping.)

Materials

- Lightweight double knitting yarn, approx. 133m (145 yards) to 50g (1.75oz), (quantities required may vary according to the yarn you choose): 4[5, 6, 8, 9] x 50g balls
- Hooks size 3mm and 3.5mm
- 1 large button
- Yarn needle

Tension

- 19 sts and 10 ½ rows to 10cm (4in) measured over rows of tr using hook size 3.5mm.
- Always check your tension carefully (see page 6), and if necessary adjust hook sizes throughout.

Sizes

Approx. age (years):

1 ½–2	2–3	4–5	6–7	8–9

To fit chest:

51	56	61	66	71cm
20	22	24	26	28in

Actual measurement:

55	61	67	73	78cm
21 ¾	24	26 ½	28 ¾	30 ¾in

Length to shoulder:

31	35.5	40	44.5	49cm
12 ¼	14	15 ¾	17 ½	19 ¼in

Sleeve seam:

20	24	31	35	39cm
8	9 ½	12 ¼	13 ¾	15 ½in

Figures in brackets [ ] refer to the four larger sizes.

1st, 2nd, 3rd and 4th sizes only

Dec row 3: 2 ch, skip first st, 1 tr in each tr to last 2 sts, 2 tr tog in last tr and 3rd of 3 ch. (1 st decreased at each end of row).

Dec row 4: as dec row 2.

1st size only

Repeat dec rows 3 and 4 once more.

All sizes

36[44, 50, 56, 64] sts. *

Repeat dec row 3, 6[10, 12, 14, 18] times in all. 24[24, 26, 28, 28] sts remain. 12[14, 16, 18, 20] raglan shaping rows in all. Fasten off.

Front

Work as given for Back to *.

Repeat dec row 3, 2[6, 6, 8, 10] times in all. 32[32, 38, 40, 44] sts remain.

Shape front neck

First side

Neck row 1: 2 ch, skip 2tr tog, 1 tr in each of next 5[5, 7, 7, 9] tr, 2 tr tog over next 2 tr, turn. Work on the remaing 6[6, 8, 8, 10] sts only.

Neck rows 2 and 3: as dec row 3. 2[2, 4, 4, 6] sts remaining.

3rd, 4th and 5th sizes only

Dec 1 st at armhole edge only on next 2[2, 4] rows.

All sizes

2 sts remain. 2 ch, skip first st, 1 tr in tr, fasten off.

Second side

With right side of Front facing, skip 16[16, 18, 20, 20] tr at centre front and rejoin yarn to next tr. Work to match first side, reversing shaping.

Sleeves (make 2)

Using hook size E (3.5mm), make 32[34, 34, 36, 36] ch.

Work rows 1 and 2 as for Back. 30[32, 32, 34, 34] sts.

Repeat row 2, twice more. 4 rows in all.

Shape sleeve

Inc row 1: 3 ch, 1 tr in first tr, 1 tr in each tr ending 2 tr in 3rd of 3 ch. 32[34, 34, 36, 36] sts. (1 st increased at each end of row.)

Be your own designer

1. Omit the button fastening and work the sweater in blocks of colour – perhaps to suit yarns from your stash. Change the edging – choose another from the Directory of edgings (see pages 66–77).

2. Choose a summery cotton yarn, add a decorative edging and flowers (Aster, page 83).

3. Add a picture – the chart for this Monkey is shown on page 63. Work the sweater Back, then work the Front to 12[10, 10, 10, 10] rows below the armhole shapings. Place the charted stitches at the center – there will be 12[15, 18, 21, 24] sts at each side of the chart. See pages 61–63 for how to use marker threads to mark the charted area. Work 12[10, 10, 10, 10] rows with the centre 28 sts worked from the chart, then shape the armholes at the same time as completing the chart in position as set.

Repeat row 2, twice. (2 rows worked without shaping.)

Repeat the last 3 rows, 4[5, 7, 8, 10] more times, and inc row 1 once again. 42[46, 50, 54, 58] sts.

Repeat row 2 until Sleeve measures 19[23, 28, 32, 37]cm / 7 ½[9, 11, 12 ½, 14 ½]in in all, ending wrong side row.

Shape raglan

Work dec row 1 as for Back. 30[34, 38, 42, 46] sts remain. Repeat dec row 3 as for Back, 10[12, 14, 16, 18] times in all. 10 sts remain.

Last row: 2 ch, skip first st, 2 tr tog over next 2 tr, 1 tr in each tr to last 3 sts, 3 tr tog over last 3 sts.

6 sts remain. 12[14, 16, 18, 20] raglan shaping rows have been worked, so matching Back and Front. Fasten off.

Assembly

Join raglan seams, matching rows carefully, and leaving top of left front raglan seam open for about 6 rows.

Join sleeve seams and side seams.

Cuffs

With right side of sleeve facing, using hook size 3mm, join yarn at sleeve seam with 1 ch, then work all around cuff edge in dc, ending 1 ss in 1 ch at beginning of round.

Work another round of dc in the same way.

Work 1 round Crab stitch as explained on page 67. Fasten off.

Lower edge

Beginning at a side seam, work as given for cuff.

Neck edge

With right side of work facing, using hook size 3mm, join yarn at top of opening (top point of left front): 1 ch, 1 dc in same place, work all around neck edge in dc, working 2 dc tog at inner corners, and ending with 2 dc tog into last 2 sts at top of left sleeve. Turn.

2nd row: 1 ch, skip 2 dc tog, 1 dc in each dc ending 2 dc in 1 ch at beginning of previous row. (1 st decreased at beginning of row, and 1 st increased at end.)

3rd row: 1 ch, 1 dc in first dc, 1 dc in each dc, ending in last dc (skipping last ch). (1 st increased at beginning of row and 1 st decreased at end).

4th row: Work in Crab stitch. Fasten off.

Opening edge and button loop

With right side of work facing, join yarn at top of right edge of opening. Work 1 row dc down to base of opening, 2 sc tog at base of opening, and 1 row dc up other side of opening to top edge. Work a button loop to fit button, as described on page 39. Fasten off.

Press or block the sweater following the instructions on the ball bands, and sew on the button to match the loop.

The aran version (left) and the lightweight double knitting version in puff stitch (right).

Pull-on hats

These hats are worked 'in the round', beginning with a circle (see page 118–119), so there are no seams to sew. Two versions of the basic pattern are given, the first in aran weight yarn, and the second in lightweight double knitting yarn.

Sizes

To fit head approx. 47.5[52.5, 57.5cm / 19 [21, 23]in. Figures in brackets [ ] refer to the two larger sizes.

Materials

- Aran weight 100% wool (approx. 76m per 50g / 48 yards per oz): 113[113, 140]g
- Optional: oddment of contrasting yarn for edging
- Hook size 5mm, or size to obtain correct tension
- Yarn needle

Tension

- 14 sts and 7 rows to 10cm (4in) measured over treble crochet.

Aran weight version

This plain hat with a turn-back brim is worked in treble crochet, and can be embellished in any way you choose.

Hat

The hat begins at centre top with a circle:

Using hook size 5mm make 5 ch, join into a ring with 1 ss in first ch made.

Round 1: 3 ch (stands for 1st tr), 11 tr into ring, 1 ss in 3rd of 3 ch. 12 tr.

Round 2: 3 ch, 1 tr in same place as base of these 3 ch, 2 tr in each tr, 1 ss in 3rd of 3 ch. 24 tr.

Round 3: 3 ch, 1 tr in same place, * 1 tr in next tr, 2 tr in next tr, * repeat from * to * ending 1 tr in last tr, 1 ss in 3rd of 3 ch. 36 tr.

Round 4: 3 ch, 1 tr in same place * 1 tr in each of next 2 tr, 2 tr in next tr, * repeat from * to * ending 1 tr in each of last 2 tr, 1 ss in 3rd of 3 ch. 48 tr.

Round 5: 3 ch, 1 tr in same place * 1 tr in each of next 3 tr, 2 tr in next tr, * repeat from * to * ending 1tr in each of 3 tr, 1 ss in 3rd of 3 ch. 60 tr.

1st size only

Next round: 3 ch, 1 tr in same place, * 1 tr in each of next 9 tr, 2 tr in next tr, * repeat from * to * ending 1 tr in each of 9 tr, 1 ss in 3rd of 3 ch. 66 tr.

2nd and 3rd sizes only

Next round: 3 ch, 1 tr in same place, * 1 tr in each of 4 tr, 2 tr in next tr, * repeat from * to * ending 1 tr in each of 4 tr, 1 ss in 3rd of 3 ch. 72 tr.

3rd size only

Foll round: 3 ch, 1 tr in same place, * 1 tr in each of 11 tr, 2 tr in next tr, * repeat from * to * ending 1 tr in each of 11 tr, 1 ss in 3rd of 3 ch. 78 tr.

All sizes

66[72, 78] tr.

Next round: 3 ch, 1 tr in each tr, ending 1 ss in 3rd of 3 ch.

Repeat this round until Hat measures 23.5[25, 26]cm / 9 ½[10, 10 ½]in from centre when laid flat, or depth required, to allow for turn-back brim. For a hat without a turn-back brim, work 6.5cm / 2 ½in less.

Fasten off. Pull gently on the starting tail to close the centre of the circle. Darn in the tails.

Add an edging

Use an oddment of contrasting yarn to add the edging of your choice: we added Blanket edging (see page 70). Remember that the brim will be turned back, so work the edging with the inside of the hat facing you.

Lightweight double knitting version

This version of the hat has no brim. After working the circular top, the unshaped rounds are worked in a puff stitch pattern.

Hat

Using hook size 4mm, begin with 5 ch and work rounds 1–5 as for worsted (aran) version, left.

Round 6: 3 ch, 1 tr in same place * 1 tr in each of next 4 tr, 2 tr in next tr, * repeat from * to * ending 1tr in each of 4 tr, 1 ss in 3rd of 3 ch. 72 tr.

Round 7: 3 ch, 1 tr in same place * 1 tr in each of next 5 tr, 2 tr in next tr, * repeat from * to * ending 1tr in each of 5 tr, 1 ss in 3rd of 3 ch. 84 tr.

2nd and 3rd sizes only

Round 8: 3 ch, 1 tr in same place * 1 tr in each of next 6 tr, 2 tr in next tr, * repeat from * to * ending 1tr in each of 6 tr, 1 ss in 3rd of 3 ch. 96 tr.

3rd size only

Round 9: 3 ch, 1 tr in same place * 1 tr in each of next 7 tr, 2 tr in next tr, * repeat from * to * ending 1tr in each of 7 tr, 1 ss in 3rd of 3 ch. 108 tr.

All sizes

84[96, 108] tr.

Next round: 3 ch, 1 tr in each tr, 1 ss in 3rd of 3 ch.

For a plain hat, repeat the last round to depth required.

For a patterned hat as shown in the photograph, work in Puff Stitch Pattern as below (or another pattern with a stitch repeat of 3, 4, 6 or 12 sts):

Puff Stitch Pattern

Special abbreviation: 1 group: [yrh, insert hook as directed, pull through a loop] 3 times in same place, yrh, pull through first 6 loops on hook, yrh, pull through remaining 2 loops.

Round 1: 1 ch, 1 dc in each of next 2 tr, * 1 ch, skip 1 tr, 1 dc in each of next 5 tr, * repeat from * to *, ending 1 dc in each of 3 tr, 1 ss in 1 ch.

Round 2: 3 ch, 1 tr in next dc, * 1 ch, skip 1 dc, 1 group in 1-ch sp, 1 ch, skip 1 dc, 1 tr in each of next 3 dc, * repeat from * to *, ending 1 tr in last dc, 1 ss in 3rd of 3 ch.

Round 3: 1 ch, 1 dc in first tr, * 1 dc in 1-ch sp, 1 ch, skip top of group, 1 dc in 1-ch sp, 1 dc in each of 3 tr, * repeat from * to *, ending 1 dc in last tr, 1 ss in 1 ch.

Repeat rounds 2 and 3 until work measures 17.5[18.5, 20]cm / 7[7 ½, 8]in from centre when laid flat, or depth required.

Edging

The hat in the photograph is finished with Large Picot edging (see page 68), worked in rounds: Change to size 3.5mm hook.

Round 1: 1 ch, 1 dc in each dc and ch sp, ending 1 ss in 1 ch.

Repeat this round twice more.

Large picot round: 1 ch, 1 dc in next dc, * 5 ch, 1 ss in top of previous dc, skip 1 dc, 1 dc in each of next 2 dc, * repeat from * to *, ending 5 ch, 1 ss in top of previous dc, skip 1 dc, 1 ss in 1 ch. Fasten off. Pull gently on the starting tail to close the centre of the circle. Darn in the tails.

Sizes

To fit head approx. 45.5[51, 56]cm / 18[20, 22]in. Figures in brackets [ ] refer to the two larger sizes.

Materials

- Lightweight double knitting 100% wool yarn, approx. 168 m per 50g / 184 yards per 1 ¾oz: 50[60, 75]g
- Hook size 4mm, or size to obtain correct tension
- Hook size 3.5mm for optional edging
- Yarn needle

Tension

- 20 sts and 10 rows to 10cm (4in) measured over treble crochet.

Be your own designer

The basic hat pattern is very versatile, and can be adapted in any number of ways:

1. Add a pompom (see page 79) or tassel (see page 81) to the crown of the hat, and substitute the edging of your choice (see Directory of Edgings, pages 66–77).

2. Embellish with a flower, star or heart motif (see pages 82–85).

3. Add beads: instead of working the puff stitch rows on the lightweight double knitting hat, substitute a simple pattern of beads. Finish with a pretty edging, such as Frilled Flowers (see page 72). The arrangement of beads shown on the chart below repeats over 6 sts and 2 rounds. See page 56 for the method of adding beads to treble crochet. As beads are added, they appear on the opposite side of the work. So the inside of the hat, as worked, will then become the right side, resulting in a slightly different overall texture.

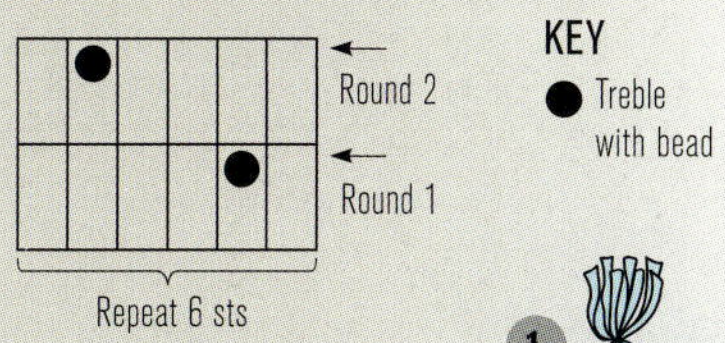

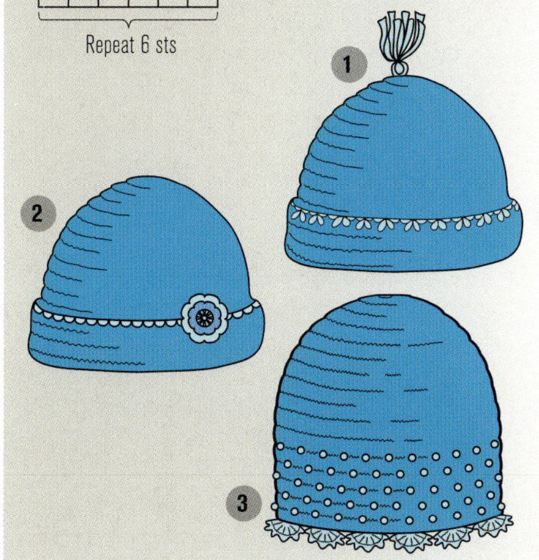

Lady's jacket

This classic jacket in a simple Shell pattern can be dressed up for special events, or worn casually with jeans and a T-shirt. Make it in your favourite colour, or ring the changes as described on page 100.

Materials

- Lightweight double knitting yarn, approx. 168m (184 yards) per 50g skein:
  Colour A (main) 9[10, 11] 50g balls
  Colour B (contrast) 1[1 1] 50g ball
- Hooks size 3.5mm and 3mm
- 5 buttons
- Yarn needle

Tension

- 4 patterns and 12 ½ rows to 10cm (4in) measured over Shell Pattern below, using size 3.5mm hook.

Sizes

To fit bust:

81–86	91–96	102–107cm
32–34	36–38	40–42in

Actual measurement:

91	102	112cm
36	40	44in

Length to shoulder:

48.5	51	53.5cm
19	20	21in

Sleeve seam:

44.5	46	47cm
17 ½	18	18 ½in

Back

Using size 3.5mm hook and colour A, make 110[122, 134] ch.

Shell Pattern

Row 1: 5 tr in 5th ch from hook, * skip 2 ch, 1 dc in next ch, skip 2 ch, 5 tr in next ch, * repeat from * to * to last 3 ch, skip 2 ch, 1 dc in last ch. 18[20, 22] shells.

Row 2 (right-side row): 5 ch, skip [1 dc, 2 tr], * 1 dc in next tr (the 3rd of 5 tr), 2 ch, skip 2 tr, 1 tr in next dc, 2 ch, skip 2 tr, * repeat from * to * ending 1 tr in 1 ch at beg previous row.

Row 3 (wrong-side row): 1 ch, skip first tr, * skip 2 ch, 5 tr in next dc, skip 2 ch, 1 dc in tr *, repeat from * to * ending 1 dc in 3rd of 5 ch.

Repeat rows 2 and 3 until Back measures 30.5[32, 33]cm / 12[12 ½, 13]in, ending row 2.

Shape armholes

**** Armhole row 1:** 1 ss in each of [2 ch, 1 dc, 2 ch, 1 tr], skip 2 ch, 5 tr in next dc, patt as set ending 1 dc in last tr (omitting last shell), turn. 16[18, 20] shells.

Armhole row 2: 1 ss in each of first 3 tr, patt as set ending 1 dc in centre tr of last shell.

Armhole row 3: 1 ss in each of [2 ch, 1 tr], patt as set ending 1 dc in last tr. ** 14[16, 18] shells.

Repeat armhole rows 2 and 3, once more.

Shell pattern

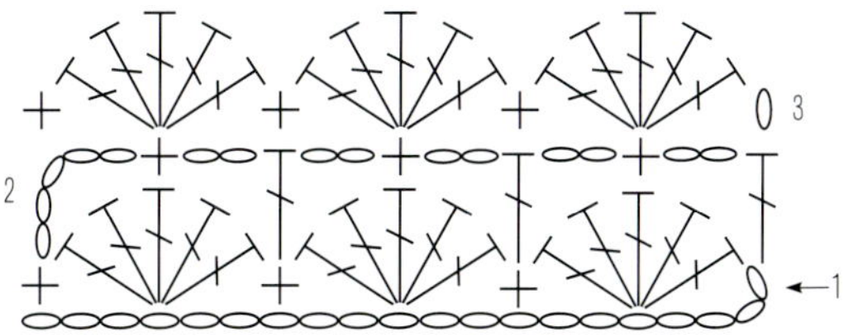

KEY
- Chain
- Double
- Treble

12[14, 16] shells remain.
Continue in Shell Pattern until Back measures 46[48.5, 51]cm / 18[19, 20]in in all, ending patt row 2.

Shape back neck

First side

Next row: Work 4[5, 5] shells as set, ending 1 dc in tr, turn.

Foll row: 1 ss in each of 3 tr, patt as set to end. Fasten off.

Second side

With right side of work facing, leave 4[4, 6] shells at centre back neck and rejoin yarn to next tr.

Next row: 1 ch, patt to end 4[5, 5] shells.

Foll row: Patt as set ending 1 dc in centre of 4th[5th, 5th] shell. Fasten off.

Left Front

Using hook size 3.5mm and colour A, make 56[62, 68] ch.
Work in Shell Pattern (9[10, 11] shells) as for Back until Front measures 30.5[32, 33]cm / 12[12 ½, 13]in, ending row 2.

Shape armhole

Armhole row 1: 1 ss in each of [2 ch, 1 dc, 2 ch, 1 tr], skip 2 ch, 5 tr in next dc, patt as set to end. 8[9, 10] shells.

Armhole row 2: Patt as set ending 1 dc in centre tr of last shell.

Armhole row 3: 1 ss in each of [2 ch, 1 tr], patt as set to end. 7[8, 9] shells.

Repeat armhole rows 2 and 3, once more.
6[7, 8] shells.
Continue in Shell Pattern until Front measures 35.5[37, 37]cm / 14[14 ½, 14 ½]in in all, ending patt row 3.

Shape neck

Neck row 1: 1 ss in each of first 3 tr, patt as set to end.

Neck row 2: Patt as set ending 1 dc in last tr (omitting last shell). 5[6, 7] shells.

Repeat these 2 rows, 2[2, 3] more times.
3[4, 4] shells.
Continue in pattern until length matches Back at shoulder edge, ending patt row 2. Fasten off.

Right Front

Using hook size 3.5mm and colour A, make 56[62, 68] ch.
Work in Shell Pattern (9[10, 11] shells) as for Back until length matches Left Front at beginning of armhole shaping, ending row 2.

Armhole row 1: Patt as set, ending 1 dc in last tr (omitting last shell). 8[9, 10] shells.

Armhole row 2: 1 ss in each of first 3 tr, patt as set to end.

Armhole row 3: Patt as set ending 1 dc in last tr. 7[8, 9] shells.

Repeat armhole rows 2 and 3, once more.
6[7, 8] shells.
Continue in Shell Pattern until length matches Left Front at beginning of front neck shaping, ending patt row 3.

Shape neck

Neck row 1: Patt as set ending 1 dc in centre of last shell.

Neck row 2: 1 ss in each of [2 ch, 1 tr], patt as set to end. 5[6, 7] shells.

Repeat these 2 rows, 2[2, 3] more times.
3[4, 4] shells.
Continue in pattern until length matches Back at shoulder edge, ending patt row 2. Fasten off.

Sleeves (make 2)

Using size 3.5mm hook and colour A, make 56[62, 68] ch.
Work in Shell Pattern (9[10, 11] shells) as for Back until Sleeve measures 16.5[17.5, 19]cm / 6 ½[7, 7 ½]in, ending patt row 3.

Shape sleeve

Inc row 1: 5 ch, 1 tr in first dc, patt as set ending [1 tr, 2 ch, 1 tr] in 1 ch.

Inc row 2: 3 ch, 2 tr in first tr, skip 2 ch, 1 dc in next tr, patt as set ending 3 tr in 3rd of 5 ch.

Inc row 3: 3 ch, skip first 3 tr, 1 tr in first dc, patt as set ending 2 ch, skip 2 tr, 1 dc in 3rd of 3 tr.

Inc row 4: 3 ch, 2 tr in first tr, skip 2 ch, 1 dc in next tr, patt as set ending 1 dc in last tr, skip 2 ch, 3 tr in next ch.

Inc row 5: 5 ch, 1 dc in first tr, patt as set ending [1 dc, 2 ch, 1 tr] in 3rd of 3 ch.

Inc row 6: 1 ch, 5 tr in first dc, patt as set ending 5 tr in last dc, 1 dc in 3rd of 5 ch.
11[12, 13] shells.

Inc rows 7–10: Work in patt as set.

Repeat these 10 rows, twice more.
15[16, 17] shells.
Continue without shaping until Sleeve measures 43[44, 5, 45.5]cm / 17[17 ½, 18]in or length required, ending patt row 3.

Shape top of sleeve

Work as given for Back armhole shaping from ** to **. 13[14, 15] shells.
Repeat armhole rows 2 and 3, 4 more times.
5[6, 7] shells remain. Fasten off.

Assembly

Join shoulder seams, matching shell patterns. Join top edges of sleeves to armholes. Join side and sleeve seams.

Cuffs

With right side of sleeve facing, using hook size 3mm, join colour B at sleeve seam. The edging is worked in rounds:

Round 1: 1 ch, work 1 dc in base of each st and group, and 2 dc in each 2-ch sp, all around, ending 1 ss in 1 ch at beginning of round.

Round 2: 1 ch, 1 dc in each dc, ending 1 ss in 1 ch.

Round 3: as round 2.

Picot round: 1 ch, skip first dc, * 3 ch, 1 ss in first of these 3 ch, skip 1 dc, 1 dc in next dc, * repeat from * to * ending 1 ss in 1 ch. (If necessary, work 2 dc tog near the end of the round to adjust the number of stitches.) Fasten off.

Front, neck and lower edges

With right side of work facing, using hook size 3mm, join colour B at right side seam.

Round 1: Work in dc along lower edge in same way as for Cuff. At corner, work [1 dc, 1 ch, 1 dc] in same place. Work in dc up right front edge, working 3 dc for every 2 rows of pattern, and working 2 dc in same place at beginning of front neck shaping. Work around neck edge in dc, working 2 dc tog at each inner corner. Work down left front edge in same way, [1 dc, 1 ch, 1 dc] in same place as corner, then all around lower edge in same way as for cuff, ending 1 ss in 1 ch at beginning of round. Mark positions for 5 buttonholes on right front edge, the top one just below the front neck shaping, and 4 more at approx. 7.5cm (3in) intervals below: count the stitches between the markers to make sure they are evenly spaced. Check the width of the buttonholes required as shown on page 38.

Round 2: 1 ch, 1 dc in each dc, working horizontal buttonholes to match markers (see page 39), and also working [1 dc, 1 ch, 1 dc] in 1-ch sp at each outer corner and 2 dc tog at each inner corner, ending 1 ss in 1 ch.

Round 3: Work in dc as round 2, completing the horizontal buttonholes.

Picot round: Work as given for cuff. Fasten off Darn in any remaining yarn tails. Sew on buttons to match buttonholes. Press or block if required.

Be your own designer

This jacket pattern can be personalised in several ways:

1. Add patch pockets (see page 35), and/or use tie fastenings (see page 37) instead of buttons and buttonholes.

2. Include isolated stripes (page 49) in contrasting colour(s), and change the edging.

3. For a lighter version of the jacket, choose a cotton yarn, and change the shell pattern to a more open version, by working '[1 tr, 1 ch] twice, 1 tr', instead of each group of 5 tr given in the jacket instructions, as follows:

Lacy shell pattern

Begin with a base chain of a multiple of 6 sts, plus 2, as given in the jacket instructions.

Special abbreviation: 1 group = [1 tr, 1 ch] twice, 1 tr, all worked in same place as given below.

Row 1: 1 group in 5th ch from hook, * skip 2 ch, 1 dc in next ch, skip 2 ch, 1 group in next ch, * repeat from * to * to last 3 ch, skip 2 ch, 1 dc in last ch. 18[20, 22] groups.

Row 2 (right-side row): 5 ch, skip [1 dc, 1 tr, 1 ch], * 1 dc in next tr, 2 ch, skip [1 ch, 1 tr], 1 tr in next dc, 2 ch, skip [1 tr, 1 ch], * repeat from * to * ending 1 tr in 1 ch at beg previous row.

Row 3 (wrong-side row): 1 ch, skip first tr, * skip 2 ch, 1 group in next dc, skip 2 ch, 1 dc in tr *, repeat from * to * ending 1 dc in 3rd of 5 ch.

When working the shapings at armholes, neck and sleeves, remember that each group is equivalent to 5 tr in the pattern instructions.

Pillow in squares

Make this pillow in any colour combination to match the scheme of your room.

Size
40 x 40cm (16 x 16in)

Materials
- Double knitting yarn (approx. 110m per 50g / 60 yards per oz):
  Colour A (mango) 3 x 50g balls
  Colour B (cream) 2 x 50g balls
  Colour C (strawberry) 1 x 50g ball
  Colour D (slate) 1 x 50g ball
  Colour E (apple) 1 x 50g ball
- Hook size 3.5mm
- Yarn needle
- Zip length 40cm (16in)
- Sewing thread to match zip
- Sewing equipment
- Pillow pad 40 x 40cm (16 x 16in)

Tension
- First 4 rounds (completed circle) should measure 9.5cm (3 ¾in) diameter, using size 3.5mm hook. This is a tighter tension than normal for this yarn, to make a firm fabric that will not sag in use.

Abbreviations
See page 123

Square 1 (make 3)
Using colour C, work 5 ch and join into a ring with 1 ss in 1st ch made.

Round 1: 3 ch (counts as 1 tr), 15 tr into ring, 1 ss in 3rd of 3 ch at beg of round. 16 tr.

Round 2: 3 ch (counts as 1 tr), 2 tr in each tr all around, 1 tr in same place as base of ch, ss in 3rd of 3 ch at beg of round. 32 tr.

Round 3: 3 ch (counts as 1 tr), [1 tr in next tr, 2 tr in foll tr] 15 times, 1 tr in same place as base of 3 ch, ss in 3rd of 3 ch at beg of round. 48 tr.

Round 4: 3 ch (counts as 1 tr), [1 tr in each of next 2 tr, 2 tr in next tr] 15 times, 1 tr in each of last 2 tr, 1 tr in same place as base of 3 ch, ss in 3rd of 3 ch at beg of round. Fasten off C. 64 tr. (Check tension here, as above.)

Join A to any tr of previous round.

Round 5: 6 ch (counts as 1 dtr, 2 ch), * 2 dtr in next tr, 1 tr in each of next 2 tr, 1 htr in each of next 2 tr, 1 dc in each of next 6 tr, 1 htr in each of next 2 tr, 1 tr in each of next 2 tr, 2 dtr in next tr, 2 ch, repeat from * to * twice more, 2 dtr in next tr, 1 tr in each of next 2 tr, 1 htr in each of next 2 tr, 1 dc in each of next 6 tr, 1 htr in each of next 2 tr, 1 tr in each of next 2 tr, 1 dtr in same place as base of 6 ch, ss in 4th of 6 ch at beg of round.

Round 6: Ss in first 2-ch sp, 5 ch (counts as 1 tr, 2 ch), 2 tr in same 2-ch sp, * 1 tr in each of next 18 sts, [2 tr, 2 ch, 2 tr] in 2-ch sp, * repeat from * to * twice more, 1 tr in each of next 18 sts, 1 tr in last ch sp, ss in 3rd of 5 ch at beg of round.

Round 7: Ss in first 2-ch sp, 3 ch (counts as 1 dc, 2 ch), 1 dc in same ch sp, * 1 dc in each of 22 tr, [1 dc, 2 ch, 1 dc] in 2-ch sp, * repeat from * to * twice more, 1 dc in each of 22 tr, fasten off with 1 ss in 1st of 3 ch at beg of round. Fasten off, leaving a 30cm (12in) tail for assembly.

Square 2 (make 3)
Work as for Square 1, but use colour D instead of colour C.

Square 3 (make 3)
Work as for Square 1, but use colour E instead of colour C.

Square 4 (make 3)
Work as for Square 1, but use colour B instead of colour A.

Square 5 (make 3)
Work as for Square 1, but use colour D instead of colour C, and colour B instead of colour A.

Square 6 (make 3)
Work as for Square 1, but use colour E instead of colour C, and colour B instead of colour A.

Assembly
Each side of the pillow consists of nine squares. Different arrangements may be made – try them out for yourself.

Decide on the arrangement you prefer. For each panel, use hook size 3.5mm and colour A to join the squares into three strips of three with a double crochet seam (page 20), then join three strips together to make a panel of nine squares.

Use colour A to work 1 round of double crochet all around each panel, working [1 dc, 2 ch, 1 dc] at each outer corner (see page 27).

With right side uppermost, pin one edge of one panel to the zip, so that the outer edge overlaps the zip teeth, and backstitch the zip in place through the base of the double crochet edging round, using matching sewing thread. Pin the other panel to the opposite edge of the zip and sew in the same way.

Use colour A to work 1 row of double crochet along the edge of one panel next to the zip.

Fold along the zip, so wrong sides are together, and row of double crochet just worked is away from you. Join colour A at one corner, through 2-ch spaces of both thicknesses. Work in double crochet all around through both thicknesses on three sides, and through one thickness only along the zip edge, working [1 dc, 2 ch, 1 dc] at each outer corner. Fasten off. Darn in all remaining yarn tails. Press according to instructions on ball bands.

Be your own designer

The crochet square used for this pillow is very versatile: try making a few in different colours from your yarn stash, to come up with your own colour scheme.

1

1. This more restricted colour scheme creates a bold, geometric pattern. You can use the square blocks to make a blanket of any size: 5 x 3 blocks shown here, or larger, as required. As a rough guide to yarn quantity, 1 x 50 g ball of double knitting yarn will make about six inner circles (rounds 1–4), and the same quantity of yarn will make the outer rounds (5–7) of about five squares.

2. Try changing colours to work different rounds of the block. You could use squares such as these to put together a multicoloured pillow or blanket, using small oddments of many different colours: be sure to choose yarns of similar weight and fibre content.

2

Felted rug

Felted woollen crochet makes a firm, substantial fabric suitable for home furnishings such as this floor rug. The felted background makes a great surface for bold embroidery.

Size

Approx. 56 x 86cm (22 x 34in)

Materials

- Aran weight 100% wool (approx. 76m per 50g / 48 yards per oz): 4oz (113g) of each colour:
  Colour A (dark blue)
  Colour B (pale blue)
  Colour C (light turquoise)
  Colour D (dark purple)
  Colour E (light purple)
  Colour F (dark turquoise)
- Oddments of woollen yarns of similar weight for embroidery (three colours are used here: peach, mango and pale gold).
- Hooks size 5mm (or size to obtain correct gauge) and 4.5mm
- Large, sharp needle (darning needle)
- Thimble
- Card for templates
- Dressmaker's chalk pencil

Tension

- After felting: 18 sts and 10 ½ rows to 10cm (4in).
- To test tension, make a sample piece 36 sts wide and 21 rows deep – this should measure approx. 25 x 25cm (10 x 10in). Felt the sample as described on page 64. Sample should then measure approx. 20 x 20cm (8 x 8in).
- Tension is not crucial if a change in size is acceptable, but a substantial amount of shrinkage is required to make a hardwearing fabric.

Abbreviations

- See page 123

Rug

Using hook size 5mm and colour A make 102 ch.

Row 1: 1 tr in 4th ch from hook, 1 tr in each ch to end. 100 tr.

Stripe Pattern

The rug is worked throughout in single-row, three-colour stripes (see page 49).

Join in colour B.

Row 2: 3 ch, sk first tr, 1 tr in each tr, ending 1 tr in 3rd of 3 ch.

Join in colour C. Work 1 row as row 2.

Using colours A, B, C in turn, work 12 more rows as row 2. Break off A and join in D.

Using colours D, B, C in turn, work 15 rows as row 2. Break off B and join in E.

Using colours D, E, C in turn, work 15 rows as row 2. Break off C and join in F.

Using colours D, E, F in turn, work 15 rows as row 2. Break off D and join in A.

Using colours A, E, F in turn, work 15 rows as row 2. Break off E and join in B.

Using colours A, B, F in turn, work 15 rows as row 2. Fasten off all colours

Edging

Using hook size 4.5mm, and colour A, work 2 rounds dc all around outside edges (see page 27). Fasten off. Run in all the yarn tails.

Felting

Felt the rug using the washing machine method described on page 64. After felting, lay the rug flat and leave to dry completely.

If the edges do not lie flat, use a large sharp needle to thread a length of matching yarn through the edging along one side. Secure one end by running the yarn back and forth through the edging for about 5cm (2in). Then pull gently on the other tail to draw up the edge slightly until it lies flat, and secure this tail in the same way. Repeat on the other edges as necessary.

Embroidery

Photocopy the design outlines onto thin card, enlarging by 200 per cent. We used three large flowers and eighteen ovals. Cut out the shapes and arrange them on the right side of the rug, following the photograph as a guide. When you are happy with the arrangement, pin each shape in place, and draw around it with the chalk pencil. Remove the card shapes.

To work the embroidery, it is best to lay the rug flat on a smooth surface. Use a thimble and a large, sharp-pointed needle (darning needle). The yarn tails may be hidden by darning them through the thickness of the felt, beneath the stitches, so they do not show through to the other side. The stitches may be worked in a similar way, running the needle through the thickness of the felt rather than taking it right through to the wrong side of the fabric.

Do not stitch too tightly. The following embroidery stitches are shown on pages 58–59:

- Using peach yarn, work the outlines of the large flowers in chain stitch, and their centres as circles of blanket stitch in pale gold.
- Use mango yarn to work about half the ovals in blanket stitch, with a circle of chain stitch in peach at the centre.
- Use pale gold to work the remaining ovals in blanket stitch. At the centres, work a star stitch in mango:

Run the yarn tail through the fabric from 1 (centre) to 2. Insert the needle at 1 and bring it out at 3. Insert it again at 1 and bring it out at 4. Repeat, bringing the needle out at 5, 6, and 7 in turn. Insert needle at 1 and bring it out below 7 to fasten off the yarn.

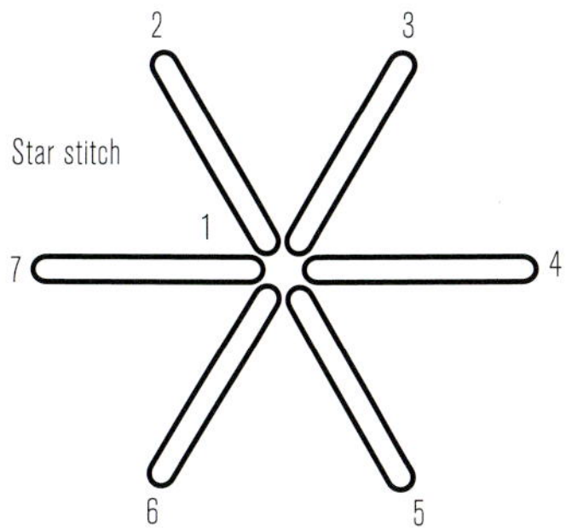

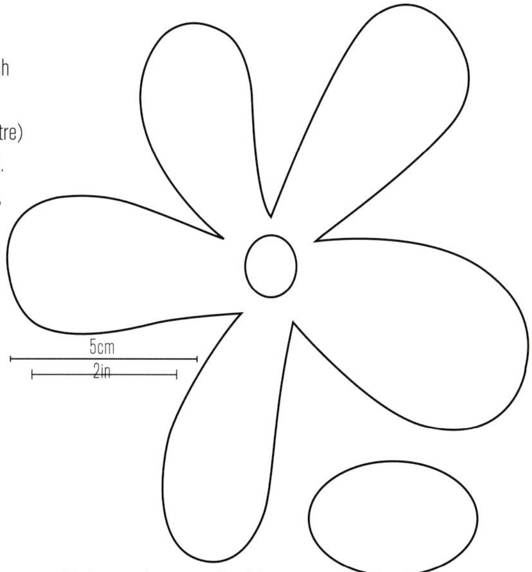

Enlarge these embroidery outlines by 200 per cent, by photocopying onto thin card.

Be your own designer

You can adapt this design in so many ways. Follow these guidelines to invent your own design:

- Make sure that the yarn you use is suitable for felting (see page 64).
- Make a sample piece (note down the hook size, number of stitches and rows) and felt it.
- Measure the felted sample.
- Calculate how many stitches and rows you need to make a rug to any measurements you want.

1. For a more traditional look, work a rug in stripes of muted colours made by combining yarns (see page 47). Here, lavender blue wool was combined with light turquoise mohair for the paler stripes, while the same lavender blue wool was combined with mid-blue mohair for the darker stripes. The blue cotton fringe was added after felting, using the method shown for the Cut fringe (see page 80), but using a sharp needle instead of a crochet hook, and the strands of the fringe were then knotted in pairs.

2. If you prefer, work the crochet piece in a single colour, then work any embroidery you like. Here, the heart outline was drawn with the aid of a template, as page 55, and the swirling line drawn by hand.

Crochet basics

Here's a brief refresher course covering the basic crochet techniques needed to follow any instructions in this book. If you're unsure about a particular stitch or method, check here for a clear, step-by-step description to help you on your way.

Starting out

You may already have a favourite way of holding the crochet hook and yarn. However, if your tension is uneven, or consistently tighter or looser than recommended tensions in pattern instructions, try the established techniques shown on this page.

Holding the hook

There are two ways to hold a crochet hook. Try them out to find which suits you best.

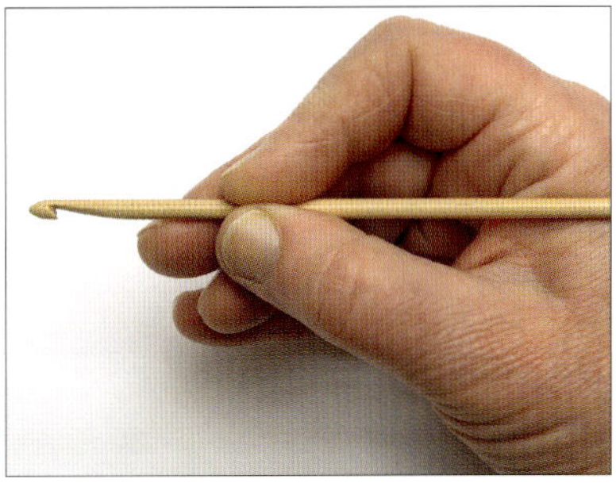

Option 1: Hold the crochet hook as you would hold a pen. This grip is often used by those who prefer making lightweight, lacy crochet.

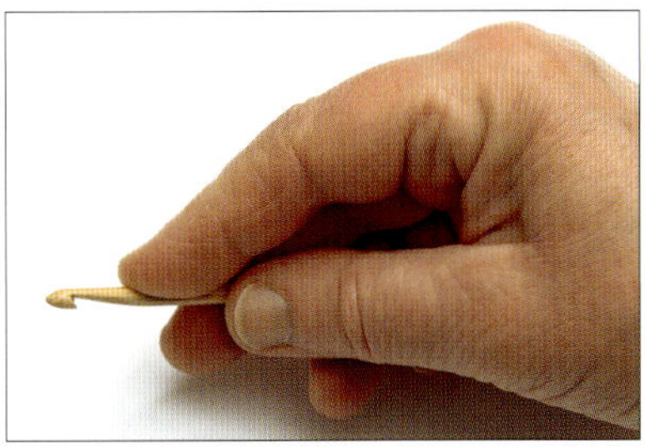

Option 2: Hold the hook as you would hold a knife. You may find this grip more suitable if you prefer working with medium to heavy-weight yarns.

Start with a slipknot

Almost every piece of crochet begins with a slipknot. The slipknot is not included when counting stitches.

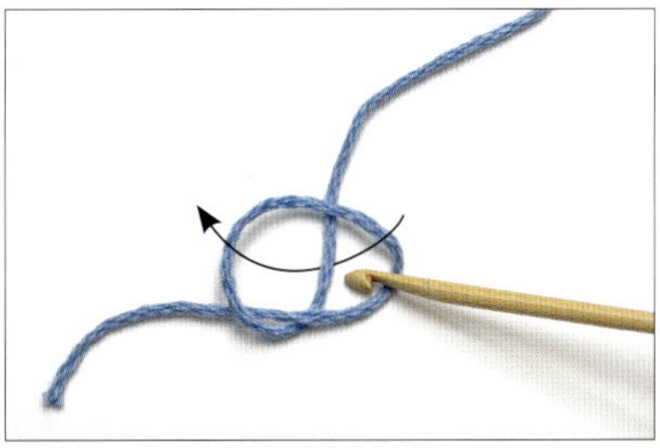

1 Loop the yarn as shown, with the short tail to the left.

2 Slide the knot onto the hook as shown. Pull on the short tail to tighten the knot gently (it should not be too tight).

IF YOU ARE LEFT HANDED

Hold this book so you can see the photographs reflected in a mirror, and read 'left hand' for 'right hand', and vice versa, throughout.

Holding the yarn

There are many different ways to hold the yarn, but the method shown here gives good control. With a little practice, it becomes easy to maintain a constant tension and produce swift, even stitches.

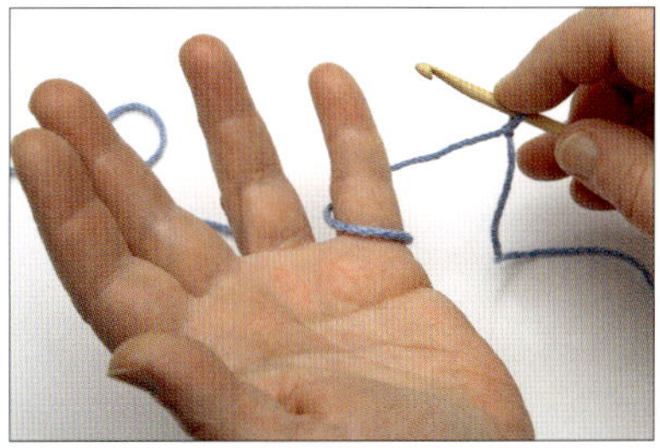

1 Hold the hook with the slipknot on it in your right hand, and catch the yarn leading to the ball with the little finger of your left hand in the direction shown.

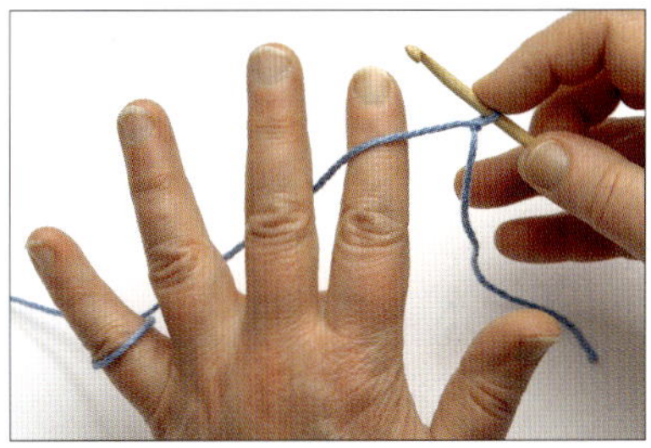

2 Turn your left hand over and slip your left forefinger under the yarn, close to the hook.

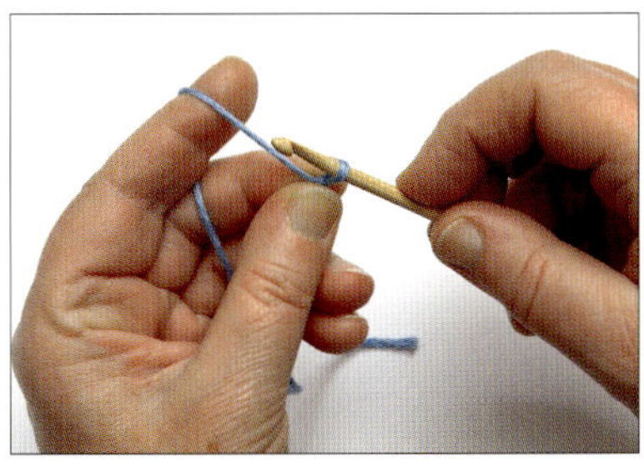

3 Use your thumb and middle finger to hold the short yarn tail just below the hook. Once work is in progress, hold the work below the hook in exactly the same way.

Basic stitches

The common stitches on which all crochet stitch patterns are based are shown on the following pages.

Chain stitch

⬭ CH, ch

Chain stitch is used to make base chains, sometimes called foundation chains (see page 13), turning chains (see page 111), and also as part of many stitch patterns.

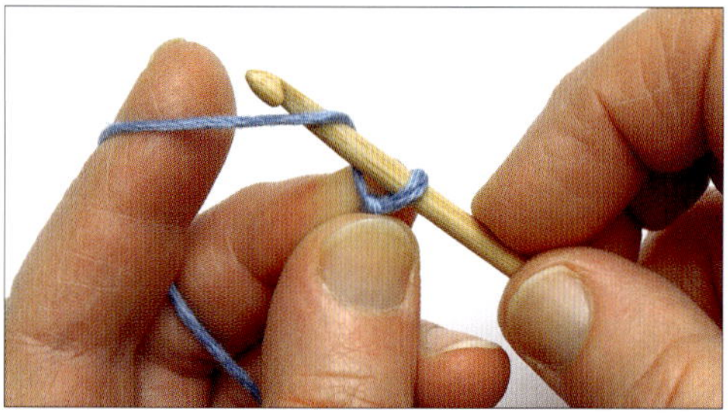

1 Catch the yarn with the hook, in the direction shown, using your left forefinger to keep the yarn tight.

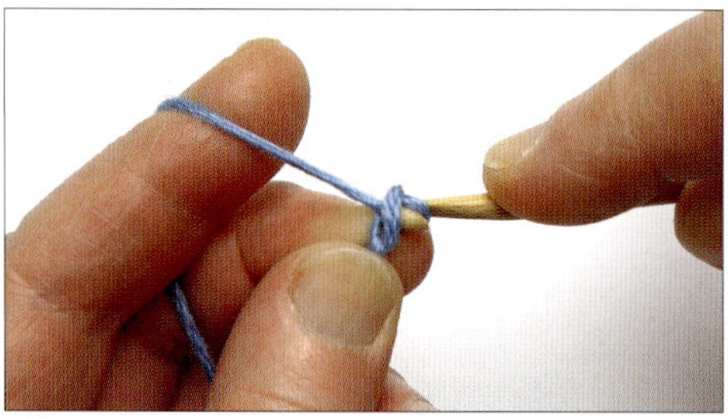

2 Pull the yarn through the loop on the hook. Allow the old loop to drop off the hook. One chain stitch is made.

3 Continue working. As the length of chains increases, shift the left hand closer to the hook every few stitches. When counting chains, do not include the slipknot or the loop on the hook.

Slip stitch

• SS, ss

This is the shallowest crochet stitch, often used for moving from one position to another without adding any substantial bulk to the work, and also as part of many stitch patterns. Rows of slip stitch make a very firm fabric, suitable for an edging.

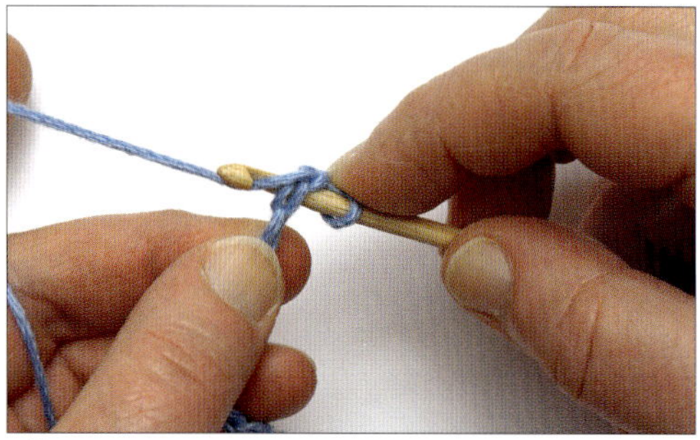

1 Insert the hook where required by the pattern instructions (shown here inserted in a base chain). Catch the yarn with the hook as shown.

2 Pull a new loop of yarn through all the loops on the hook. One slip stitch is made.

3 Repeating steps 1 and 2 in every chain makes a row of slip stitch.

Double crochet

+ DC, dc

This is a very common stitch. Rows of double crochet make a plain, firm fabric, and the stitch is also used as an element of many stitch patterns.

1 To work along a base chain, insert the hook in the second chain from the hook. Catch the yarn and pull a new loop through the chain only, making 2 loops on the hook.

2 Catch the yarn again, and pull it through both loops on the hook.

3 To make a row of double crochet, repeat steps 1 and 2 in every chain.

WORKING FURTHER ROWS OF DOUBLE CROCHET

There are two ways to work rows of double crochet: the American method and the English method. If you are confused by pattern instructions that include double crochet, make small sample pieces to try out the pattern twice, once for each method below.

AMERICAN METHOD

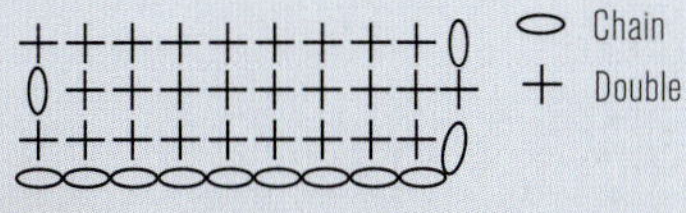

1 At the beginning of a row, work 1 turning chain, skip the last stitch of the previous row, and insert the hook into the second stitch. The chain is counted as the first stitch of the row.

2 Pull through a loop of yarn and complete the double crochet stitch as before. At the end of a row, work 1 double crochet into the turning chain at the beginning of the previous row.

ENGLISH METHOD

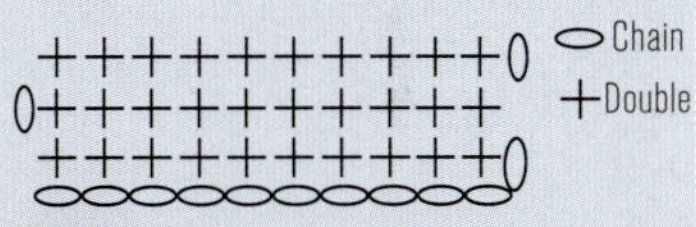

1 At the beginning of a row, work 1 turning chain, and insert the hook into the last stitch of the previous row. The turning chain is not counted as a stitch.

2 Pull through a loop and complete the stitch. At the end of a row, work the last stitch into the first stitch of the previous row – DO NOT work into the turning chain.

WHERE TO INSERT THE HOOK

- When you are working in rows, whatever the stitch, the top of the stitch last made is at 1, just behind the hook, to the right of the stem of the stitch.

- Therefore, when you turn the work at the end of a row, the top of the last stitch is at 2. For most basic stitches worked in rows, this stitch is skipped, and one or more turning chains are worked to count as the first stitch of the new row. Unless otherwise specified, to work the next stitch, the hook is inserted at 3.

Half-treble crochet

T HTR, htr

This stitch is taller than double crochet. When worked in rows, it produces a firm fabric, and grows more quickly than double crochet.

1 Wrap the yarn over the hook. When working into a base chain, insert the hook into the third chain from the hook (the first 2 chain count as the first stitch of the row). Otherwise, insert the hook where directed. Catch the yarn again and pull a new loop through the base chain (or the work) only, making three loops on the hook.

2 Catch the yarn again and draw it through all three loops on the hook. One half-treble crochet has been made.

3 Repeat steps 1 and 2 to work a row of half-treble crochet. On following rows, begin with 2 chain, skip the last stitch of the previous row, and work the last st into the second of 2 ch at the beginning of the previous row.

Treble crochet

 TR, tr

This stitch is taller than a half-treble crochet stitch. When worked in rows, it forms a softly draping fabric that grows quickly.

1 Wrap the yarn over the hook. To work into a base chain, insert the hook in the fourth chain from the hook (the first 3 chain count as the first stitch of the row) – otherwise, insert the hook where directed.

2 Catch the yarn with the hook and pull a loop through, making three loops on the hook. Catch the yarn again.

3 Pull the yarn through the first two loops on the hook. Two loops remain on the hook.

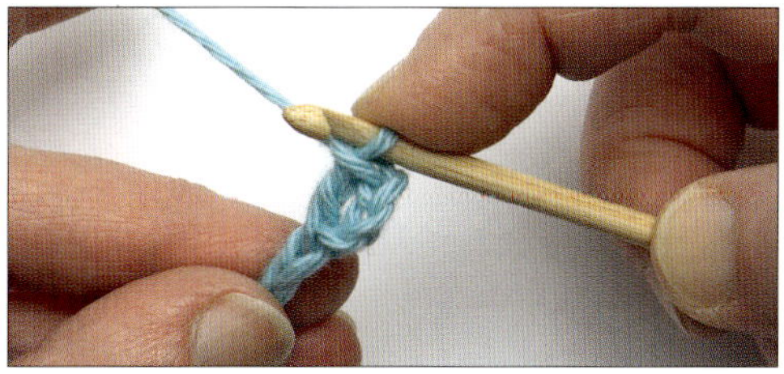

4 Catch the yarn again and pull it through the remaining two loops on the hook. One treble crochet has been made.

5 Repeat steps 1–4 to form a row of treble crochet. On following rows, begin with 3 ch, skip the last tr of the previous row, and work the last tr into the third of 3 ch at beginning of previous row.

QUICK GUIDE TO TURNING CHAINS

To begin a row of crochet, work the required number of turning chains as below and skip the top of the last stitch of the previous row (unless you are working double crochet rows by the English method, see page 109).

To end a row of crochet, work the last stitch into the last turning chain at the beginning of the previous row.

Confusingly, different names are used for some crochet stitches in the United States and in the United Kingdom. If you come across a stitch pattern that doesn't seem to make sense, consider whether this difference in terminology may be the problem. The number of turning chains given for beginning a row can provide the clue.

US	UK	Turning chains at beginning of row
single crochet (sc)	double crochet (dc)	1ch
half-double (hdc)	half treble (htr)	2ch
double crochet (dc)	treble (tr)	3ch
treble (tr)	double treble (dtr)	4ch
double treble (dtr)	triple treble (ttr) or long treble (ltr)	5ch

Double treble crochet

DTR, dtr

This stitch forms a fairly loose fabric when worked in rows, and is often used in combination with other stitches to form stitch patterns.

1 Wrap the yarn twice around the hook. To work into a base chain, insert the hook into the fifth chain from the hook (the first 4 ch count as the first tr of the row). Otherwise, insert the hook as directed.

2 Catch the yarn and pull a new loop through the base chain (or through the work) only, making four loops on the hook.

3 Catch the yarn and pull it through the first two loops on the hook, making three loops on the hook.

4 Catch the yarn again and pull it through the first two loops on the hook, making two loops on the hook.

5 Catch the yarn once more and pull it through both loops on the hook.

6 Repeat steps 1–5 to form a row of double treble crochet. On following rows, begin with 4 ch, skip the last dtr of the previous row, and at the end of the row, work the last dtr into the fourth of 4 ch at beginning of previous row.

LONG TREBLES

A triple treble (or an even longer stitch) may be made in a similar way to a double treble, above. At step 1, wrap the yarn three, four or more times around the hook. Work step 2, then repeat step 3 as many times as necessary, until two loops remain on the hook. Work step 5 to complete the long treble.
For any long treble, the number of turning chains required at the beginning of a row is two more than the number of times the yarn is wrapped around the hook.

To fasten off

When a piece of crochet is complete, it needs to be fastened off securely. You may also need to fasten off when you reach the end of a ball of yarn, before joining in another ball.

1 To fasten off your work, cut the yarn leaving a tail of at least 10cm (4in), or longer, if it will be useful for sewing a seam. Catch the yarn with the hook.

2 Pull the tail through the last loop on the hook, tightening gently. The yarn tail may be used to sew a seam, or darned in (see page 18).

To join in

There are two ways of joining in a new ball or colour. Method 1 is more secure, but method 2 is less bulky and useful when working in stripes (see pages 48–51). The technique of enclosing the yarn tails may be used to avoid having to darn the tails in later, unless you want to leave long tails for assembly.

Method 1

1 Fasten off the old yarn as above. Insert the hook where required and pull through a loop of the new yarn, leaving a tail about 10cm (4in) long.

2 Work the number of turning chain required for the stitch you are using (1 ch shown here, for double crochet).

3 Lay the yarn tail(s) across the top of the previous row, and work the first few stitches of the next row so that the tails are enclosed for about 5cm (2in). Leave the remaining lengths of tails at the wrong side of the work. When work is complete, pull gently on the tails to settle the stitches, then snip them off short.

Method 2

1 At the end of a row, drop the old yarn and work the last 'yarn round hook, pull through' of the last stitch in the new yarn, leaving a tail of about 10cm (4in).

2 Work the next row in the usual way, enclosing the yarn tails in the same way as step 3, above.

TIP

If possible, always join in a new ball at the side edge of the work. When you think you have enough yarn left for two or three more rows, * tie a loose overhand knot at the centre of the remaining length of yarn. Work 1 row. * If you reach the knot before the end of the row, you don't have enough yarn left for another row. If you don't reach the knot, untie it and repeat from * to *.

Different ways to insert the hook

The exact place where the hook is inserted to work a stitch can be varied to give different effects. Working into the front or back loops produces a flexible, ridged fabric. Front- and back-raised stitches produce firm, textured fabrics.

Working into the front loop

Whether you are working a right-side or wrong-side row, the front loop of a stitch is the thread at the top of a stitch nearest to you as you work.

Simply insert the hook under the front loop only, instead of under both threads, and work the required stitch in the usual way.

Working into the back loop

The back loop of the stitch is the thread that is furthest from you as you work the row.

Insert the hook under the back loop only – instead of under both threads – to work the required stitch.

Front-raised stitches

Inserting the hook as shown, from the front, behind the stem of the stitch and through to the front again, makes a 'front-raised' stitch (front-raised tr shown here).

Work the new stitch itself in the usual way.

Back-raised stitches

For a 'back-raised' stitch, insert the hook from the back, around in front of the stem of the stitch, and through to the back again.

Work into a chain space

Insert the hook into the space below the chain stitch(es), not the chains themselves.

RIDGE STITCHES

Working into the back loop on right-side rows, and the front loop on wrong-side rows, produces a ridged fabric, shown here in treble crochet.

RAISED STITCHES

Interesting ribbed effects can be produced by working front- and back-raised stitches in various arrangements.

OPENWORK STITCHES

Many openwork patterns, filet crochet (see page 52–53) and mesh stitches include stitches worked into chain spaces.

Grouped stitches

Stitches may be grouped together in several ways. The commonest forms are clusters, fans (or shells), puffs and popcorns.

Cluster

A cluster is worked by joining several treble crochet stitches (or longer stitches) together at the top, in the same way as for decreasing (see page 14). (3 trtog shown here.) A cluster is often followed by a chain stitch, which completes the group neatly, and on the following row a neater result may be obtained by working into this chain, or into the chain space, rather than into the top of the cluster itself.

Fan

By working several stitches into the same place, a fan or shell is produced.

Stitches are normally skipped at either side of the fan to compensate.

Puff

A puff is similar to a cluster, but is usually formed of several half-trebles, and often worked on wrong-side rows, making a puffier appearance.

1 Work * yrh, insert where required, yrh, pull through a loop *, repeat * to * the number of times required, thus making two loops on the hook for every repeat.

2 Complete the puff by working yrh, pulling through all loops on the hook. You may need to hold the work firmly with your left hand to move the hook smoothly through all the loops.

Popcorn

A popcorn is a group of several treble crochet (or longer stitches), worked into the same place, then joined at the top by linking the first stitch in the group to the last.

1 Work several stitches in the same place (4 tr shown here). Withdraw the hook from the working loop, and reinsert it either through the top of the first stitch of the group, or in the stitch before the first stitch of the group (or otherwise, if directed by pattern instructions). Catch the working loop.

2 Draw the working loop through, to close the top of the popcorn.

Reverse double crochet

This is the stitch used for the two edgings shown on page 67. It is worked from left to right, giving a neat twist to each stitch.

Insert the hook in the next stitch to the right, under the two top threads as usual. Turning the hook slightly downwards, catch the yarn and pull the loop through. (There are two loops on the hook.) Wrap the yarn around the hook in the usual direction. Pull a new loop through both the loops on the hook to complete the reverse double crochet stitch.

Picots

A picot is a little loop of chain stitches, which forms a bump, either along an edging or as part of a stitch pattern. There are two main ways in which the picot loops may be closed. Method 1 makes a picot that sits neatly on top of a stitch. Method 2 makes a rather looser effect, and the picot sits over a skipped stitch.

Method 1

1 At the position required, work a number of chains (three shown here). Insert the hook through the top of the stitch at the base of the chains to close the picot loop with a slip stitch.

2 After working the next stitch, the picot sits on top of the previous stitch.

Method 2

1 After working the required number of chains, insert the hook through the first of these chains and work 1 slip stitch to close the picot.

2 Skip one stitch before working the next stitch.

3 The picot then sits on top of the skipped stitch.

Spike stitches

Edgings using spike stitches are shown on page 70. The depth of the spikes should be adjusted to suit the main fabric: on an upper or lower edge, insert the hook 1 or 2 rows below the stitch position; on a side edge, 1 or 2 sts in from the edge.

1 Insert the hook where required (shown here 2 rows below the edge), catch the yarn and pull the loop through, up to the height of the edge (two loops on hook).

2 Insert the hook into next stitch as usual, yrh, and pull the loop through (there are three loops on hook).

3 Yrh and pull through three loops on hook to complete the spike stitch.

Extended double crochet

EXDC, exdc

When worked in rows, this stitch produces a more flexible fabric than double crochet, but its main use is to make a step increase at the end of a row (see page 15).

1 Insert the hook where required (shown here in the base of the previous stitch, at the end of a row). Pull through a loop, making two loops on the hook.

2 Catch the yarn and pull it through the first loop only.

3 Catch the yarn again and pull it through both loops on the hook to complete the stitch. To make a step increase, * insert the hook into the base of the previous stitch, repeat steps 1–3, * repeat from * to * as required. Here, three extended double crochet stitches have been added at the end of a row.

Working in the round

Crochet worked in rounds without shaping will form a tube. Rounds can also be used to make shapes such as flat circles, by increasing evenly on every round. If such increases are grouped together to make corners, then shapes such as squares and hexagons will result. Rounds of crochet may also be used to construct a border with no seams, all around an item such as a throw.

To work a tube

1 Begin a tube with a ring of chain stitches of the required size (as step 1, opposite), closed with a slip stitch. Work the number of chains equivalent to the turning chains for the stitch required (e.g. 3 ch to count as 1 tr), then work 1 st into each chain all around, ending with 1 ss into top of ch at the beginning of the round.

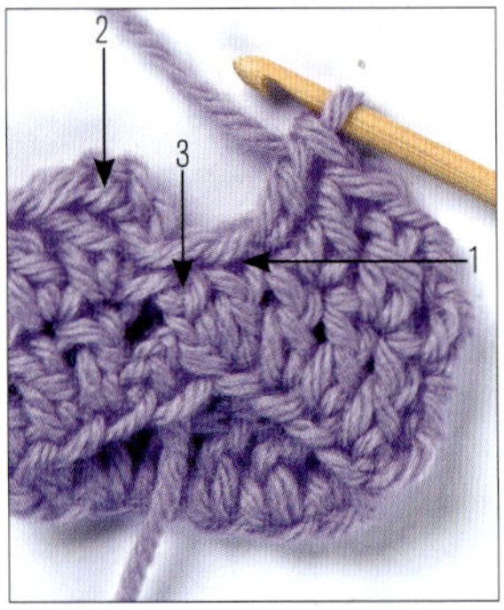

2 To avoid making unwanted increases, count the stitches carefully. At the end of each round, the last stitch is worked at (1), followed by a slip stitch into the top of the ch as above, (2). Do not work into the loop at the base of the chain, (3), or you will make an extra stitch.

3 This little tube is worked in treble crochet. Note that the joins of the rounds are in a straight vertical line.

To work a circle

The exact number of stitches required for a circle to be flat depends on the tension and stitch in use.

Instructions for a typical circle in trebles: Make 6 ch, join to ring. (Step 1, opposite).

Round 1: 3 ch, 15 tr into ring, 1 ss in 3rd of 3 ch. Count as 16 tr. (Steps 2, 3 and 4).

Round 2: 3 ch, 2 tr in each tr, ending 1 tr in same place as base of 3 ch, ss in 3rd of 3 ch. 16 incs made = 32 tr. (Step 5.)

Round 3: 3 ch, * 1 tr in next tr, 2 tr in foll tr, * repeat from * to * ending 1 tr in last tr, 1 tr in same place as base of 3 ch, ss in 3rd of 3 ch. 16 incs made = 48 tr.

Round 4: 3 ch, * 1 tr in each of next 2 tr, 2 tr in next tr, repeat from * to * ending 1 tr in each of last 2 tr, 1 tr in same place as base of 3 ch, ss in 3rd of 3 ch. 16 incs made = 64 tr. (Step 6.)

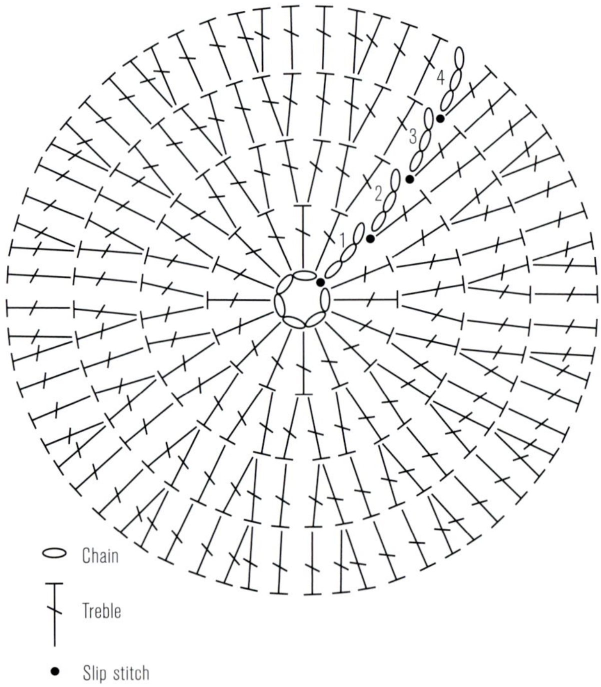

UNDERSTANDING ROUNDS

- When working in rounds, the work is not turned, so the stitches of the previous round face in the same direction as the stitches you are working.
- The top of each stitch is to the right of its stem. (Compare this with the information on Different ways to insert the hook on page 114.)

1 It is usual to begin with a ring of chain stitches. Work the number of chain stitches required, then work 1 slip stitch (see page 108) into the first chain made (not into the slipknot).

2 To begin any round, first work a number of chains, equivalent to the turning chains required for the stitch in use. These chains are counted as the first stitch of the round.

3 The first round is normally worked into the centre of the ring, not into the individual chain stitches. At the same time, you can enclose the starting tail as shown.

4 Work the number of stitches required – the number depends on the tension and the stitch in use. To close the circle, work a slip stitch into the top of the chains at the beginning of the round.

5 The second round is shown here, with 2 tr worked into every tr of the first round. Usually, the stitches are doubled on this round.

6 On the following rounds, the same number of sts is increased on every round. Placing the increases as given for rounds three and four (at left), means that the 3 ch at the beginning of the round, and the last tr of the same round, are worked into the same place and count as an increase. This makes for the neatest possible finish where the rounds are joined.

A neat finish for rounds

1 For a perfect finish at the end of any piece worked in rounds, do not close the final round. Cut the yarn leaving a 10cm (4in) tail, pull it through the last stitch, and thread it into a yarn needle. Pass the needle under the top of the first stitch of the round as shown, and back through the last stitch.

2 When tightened, the final stitch matches the others more closely.

3 On the wrong side, pull up the starting tail to close the centre, thread it into a yarn needle, and darn it in to secure.

To work a flat square

A square may be made in a similar way to a circle, but the increases are grouped together to form the four corners. The most inconspicuous place to join the rounds is on the last stitch before a corner, as given below.

When working into the stitches along each side, refer to the box on page 118 – the top of the first stitch after a chain space is the loop to the right of that stitch.

Instructions for a typical square in trebles: Make 6 ch, join to ring (as Step 1, page 119).

Round 1: 5 ch (count as 1 tr, 2 ch), [3 tr into ring, 2 ch] 3 times, 2 tr into ring, ss in 3rd of 5 ch. Each side of square = 3 tr, with 2-ch sp at each corner.

Round 2: Ss into 2-ch sp, 5 ch, 2 tr in same 2-ch sp, * 1 tr in each of 3 tr, [2 tr, 2 ch, 2 tr] in 2-ch sp, * repeat from * to * twice more, 1 tr in each of 3 tr, 1 tr in 2-ch sp at beg of round, ss in 3rd of 5 ch. Each side of square = 7 tr, with 2-ch sp at each corner.

Round 3: Ss in 2-ch sp, 5 ch, 2 tr in same 2-ch sp, * 1 tr in each tr to 2-ch sp, [2 tr, 2 ch, 2 tr] in 2-ch sp, * repeat from * to * twice more, 1 tr in each tr to 2-ch sp, 1 tr in 2-ch sp, ss in 3rd of 5 ch. Each side of square = 11 tr, with 2-ch sp at each corner.

Repeat round 3 as many times as required, thus adding 4 tr at each corner on every round.

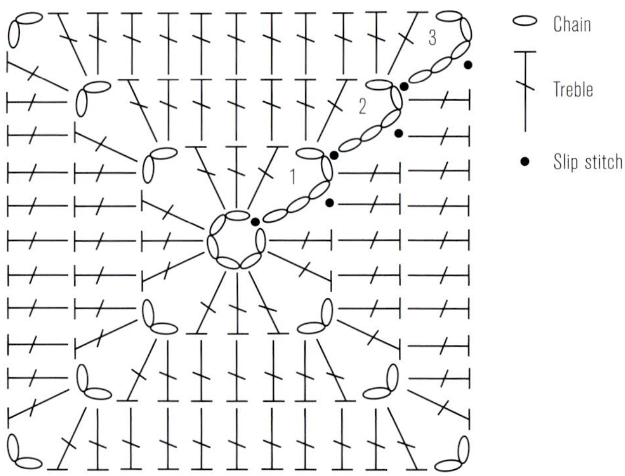

To work a hexagon

Flat medallions with five, six or more sides may also be worked in rounds, grouping the increases to form the corners. As for a square, the best place to join the rounds is just before a corner, and care should be taken when working into the first stitch after a corner (see box, page 118).

Instructions for a typical hexagon in trebles: Make 6 ch, join to ring (as Step 1, page 119).
Round 1: 5 ch (count as 1 tr, 2 ch), [2 tr into ring, 2 ch] 5 times, 1 tr into ring, ss in 3rd of 5 ch. Each side of hexagon = 2 tr, with 2-ch sp at each corner.
Round 2: Ss into 2-ch sp, 5 ch, 1 tr in same 2-ch sp, * 1 tr in each of 2 tr, [1 tr, 2 ch, 1 tr] in 2-ch sp, * repeat from * to * 4 more times, 1 tr in each of 2 tr, ss in 3rd of 5 ch. Each side of hexagon = 4 tr, with 2-ch sp at each corner.
Round 3: Ss in 2-ch sp, 5 ch, 1 tr in same 2-ch sp, * 1 tr in each tr to 2-ch sp, [1 tr, 2 ch, 1 tr] in 2-ch sp, * repeat from * to * 4 more times, 1 tr in each tr to 2-ch sp, ss in 3rd of 5 ch. Each side of hexagon = 6 tr, with 2-ch sp at each corner.
Repeat round 3 as many times as required, thus adding 2 tr at each of 6 corners on every round.

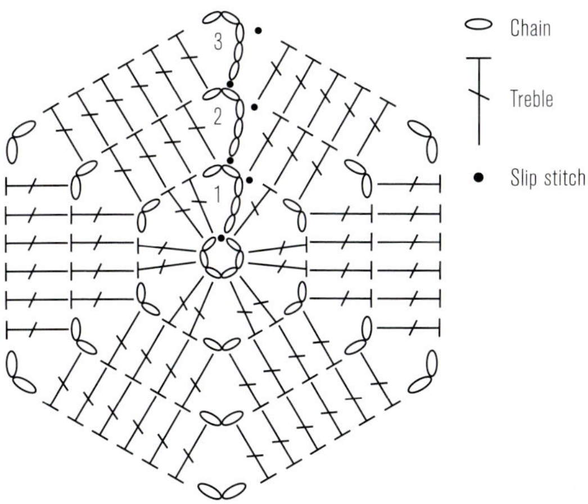

Joining hexagons

1 If you want to join hexagons with a sewn seam (see page 19), leave a long tail at the end of each hexagon. Lay out all the hexagons in the correct order before you start. Use the existing yarn tails to join the hexagons into strips (see right).

2 Then fit the strips together and sew the remaining zigzag seam in the same way. The hexagons at left were joined with a flat woven seam, worked from the right side, matching the corners exactly.

Following pattern instructions

UK crochet terminology is used throughout this book (see box, below). The style of any written instructions will vary with the publication, but the following general rules will help you understand the process.

Repeating patterns

Some basic stitch patterns may be worked over any number of stitches, but repeating patterns require a multiple of a certain number, often with a few extra to make neat edges, e.g. 'multiple of 3 sts, + 2' means any number that divides by 3, with 2 more added, such as 9 + 2 (= 11) or 33 + 2 (= 35).

One or more additional stitches are usually required for the base chain, e.g. 'multiple of 3 sts, + 2 (add 2 for base ch)' means begin with a number of base chain that divides by 3, add 2, then add 2 more, such as 33 + 2 + 2 (= 37).

Unless otherwise stated, all stitch patterns in this book begin with a right-side row.

Rows are repeated as given at the end of the instructions.

Brackets and asterisks

Instructions in brackets '[ ]' or '( )' are grouped together for one of three reasons:

1. To be read as a phrase together, e.g. 'skip [1 dc and 1 tr]' means skip 1 dc, skip 1 tr.
2. To be repeated as given after the brackets, e.g. '[2 tr in next tr, 1 ch] twice' means 2 tr in next tr, 1 ch, 2 tr in following tr, 1 ch.
3. To be worked together in the position given after the brackets, e.g. '[1 tr, 2 dc] in next dc' means 1 tr and 2 dc, all worked into the same dc.

More general instructions may also be shown in brackets, e.g. 1 tr in next tr (the centre tr of 5) helps you to position the stitch correctly.

Asterisks * are used to indicate the point from which instructions are repeated, either along a whole row, or just the number of times given, e.g. 'Repeat from * to end' means to repeat the instructions given after the *, over and over to the end of the row or round (they should fit exactly), whereas '1 ch, * 1 dc in next ch, 1 tr in next ch, repeat from * once more' means '1 ch, 1 dc in next ch, 1 tr in next ch, 1 dc in next ch, 1 tr in next ch'.

Where the instructions given after the * do not fit exactly, or if a different stitch is worked at the end of the row, the instructions may read, for example, '* 1 dc in next dc, 1 ch, skip 1 dc, 2 tr in next dc, repeat from * ending 1 tr in last dc'. This means, repeat the instructions after the *, over and over, but at the end of the last repeat, work only 1 tr in the last dc.

Asterisks and brackets may be used together, e.g. '* [1 dc in next ch, 1 tr in next ch] twice, 1 dtr in next ch, repeat from * to end' means '1 dc in next ch, 1 tr in next ch, 1 dc in next ch, 1 tr in next ch, 1 dtr in next ch, then repeat these five stitches over and over to the end of the row'.

UK/U.S. terminology

Some U.S. terms differ from the UK system, as shown below – patterns published using American terminology can be very confusing unless you understand the difference.

U.S. TERM	UK TERM	SYMBOL
single crochet	double crochet	+
half double	half treble	
double	treble	
treble	double treble	

Abbreviations and symbols

There is no worldwide standard for crochet abbreviations and symbols, but below is a list of those in common use.

COMMON ABBREVIATIONS AND SYMBOLS

Abbreviations and symbols may vary from one pattern publisher to another, so always check that you understand the system in use before commencing work.

STITCH OR TERM	ABBREVIATION	SYMBOL	
chain	CH, ch	○	
slip stitch	SS, ss	•	
double crochet	DC, dc	+	
extended double crochet	EXDC, exdc		
half treble	HTR, htr		
treble	TR, tr		
double treble	DTR, dtr		
triple treble	TTR, ttr		
chain space	ch sp	(none)	
together	TOG, tog	(none)	
yarn round hook	yrh	(none)	
group	GP, gp	(none)	
cluster	CL, cl		e.g. cluster of 3 trebles
puff stitch	PS, ps		e.g. puff of 4 half trebles
popcorn	PC, pc or P, p		e.g. popcorn of 5 trebles
reverse double crochet	REV DC, rev dc	(none)	
pattern	patt	(none)	
beginning	beg	(none)	
following	foll	(none)	
alternate	alt	(none)	

NOTES

- Sometimes special abbreviations may be used, e.g. 'SCL' or 'scl' for spike cluster, and 'RP' or 'rp' for raised popcorn.
- Any published pattern should include a list of all the abbreviations used, which may differ from those given.

Reading stitch diagrams

Always read the stitch diagram together with the text – the diagram represents how a stitch pattern is constructed, and may not bear much resemblance to the actual appearance of the finished stitch. A stitch diagram represents the right side of the work.

Rows are numbered, normally beginning with row 1 at the bottom. Right-side rows are numbered at the right, and read from right to left. Wrong-side rows are numbered at the left, and read from left to right. For patterns worked in rounds, each round is usually numbered close to where it begins, and should be read anti-clockwise, corresponding to the direction of work.

Arrangements of symbols

SYMBOLS JOINED AT TOP

A group of symbols may be joined at the top, indicating that these stitches should be worked together at the top.

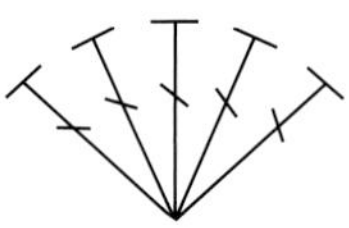

SYMBOLS JOINED AT BASE

Symbols joined at the base should all be worked into the same stitch below.

SYMBOLS JOINED AT TOP AND BASE

Sometimes a group of stitches are joined at both top and bottom, making a puff, bobble or popcorn.

SYMBOLS ON A CURVE

Sometimes symbols are drawn at an angle, depending on the construction of the stitch pattern.

DISTORTED SYMBOLS

Some symbols may be lengthened, curved or spiked, to indicate where the hook is inserted below.

Additional symbols

These are used on some charts to help make the meaning clear.

DESCRIPTION	SYMBOL
starting point	▲
join in new yarn	▽
fasten off yarn	▼
direction of working	→
do not turn work	
stitch worked in front loop only e.g.	
stitch worked in back loop only e.g.	

CARING FOR CROCHET

- Ball bands usually carry all the necessary information, and may recommend hand washing, dry cleaning or machine washing.
- Save a ball band from each type of yarn used for future reference. Where several yarns are included in one project, use the most gentle process recommended.
- If an item needs repairing, do this before washing or dry cleaning.
- If an item is stained, spot-treat the stain before washing.
- If in doubt about the best method to use, test any process on a tension swatch that includes all the yarns used for a project.
- Fasten all buttons or other fastenings. Pocket openings and front bands may also be tacked closed, so they cannot stretch out of shape.
- To wash by hand, wash by the same method shown on page 24 for blocking, and dry flat in the same way.
- Crochet garments should never be stored on clothes hangers, or they may stretch out of shape. Fold them loosely and store in a drawer or box, away from dust, damp and direct sunlight.

Now bend the rules!

Crochet is a flexible art, and once you are familiar with the ins and outs – stitches, shaping, seams and edgings – you can create completely original pieces without following detailed pattern instructions. This way of working crochet is called freeform crochet, and it's great fun to try.

A simple project

For your first experiment, choose a simple shape, such as a square pillow, or a rectangular baby blanket. Select oddments of suitable yarns from your stash: it helps if the yarns are all of similar weight and fibre content. Choose a combination of colours that pleases you (if in doubt, try matching the colours to, say, a favourite printed fabric, or perhaps a picture).

1 Make a paper pattern the exact size of the crochet piece(s) you need. Squared paper as shown here is very useful, but you can use plain paper – draw the required shape as accurately as possible. The photo shows a 35cm (14in) square paper pattern for a pillow panel. Keep the pattern to hand as you work, pinned flat on a board.

Begin by making several 7.5–10cm (3–4in) squares, rectangles or triangles in different colours and stitches – experiment with stripes and textured stitch patterns too. Move them around on your paper pattern and arrange them as you wish. Pieces may be joined with sewn or crochet seams, or worked directly onto the edge of previous pieces. Make more pieces to complete the required shape, which should lie as flat as possible on the paper pattern.

2 When the panel is complete, block it carefully to size (see page 24). Weaving (see page 54), surface crochet (see page 55), embroidery (see pages 58–59), or other embellishments can be used to firm up loose areas, and also to balance the composition.

For a pillow, make another panel of the same size (any suitable colour and stitch) for the back, and assemble with a zip in the same way as the pillow on page 102.

Add an edging or border of your choice. This pillow is finished with a Corkscrew fringe (see page 77).

Glossary

Back (of work)
The side of the work facing away from you as you work the current row or round.

Backstitch
A sewn stitch used for assembly (see page 19), and also in embroidery (see page 58).

Base chain
(Foundation chain). The initial length of chain stitches used to begin most crochet work.

Blanket stitch
An embroidery stitch (see page 59).

Block
A square, hexagon or other regular shape, designed to be repeated and assembled in multiples, patchwork-style.

Blocking
Washing (or wetting) crochet, then pinning it to shape while it dries, to fix the shape and settle the stitches (see page 24).

Bobble
Several stitches worked in the same place and joined together at the top, often on a background of shorter stitches

Border
An edging that is worked separately and sewn in place.

Chain
A crochet stitch (see page 108), or an embroidery stitch (see page 58).

Chevron
A zigzag formation of stitches.

Cluster
Several stitches worked together at the top (see page 115).

Collar stand
Shaped rows added to a neck edge before adding a collar, to add extra depth at the back of the neck (see page 32).

Cotton
Yarn spun from the fibres of cotton plants.

Crochet
A continuous thread worked into a fabric of interlocking loops with the aid of a hook, and the act of working such a fabric.

Edge treatment
An edging worked directly onto the main piece of crochet.

Edging
General term for any type of edging: either a border, or an edge treatment.

Eyelet
A small hole worked in the crochet, for a buttonhole or drawstring, or as part of a lace pattern.

Fan
Several stitches worked into the same place, so joined at the base to make a fan (or shell) formation (see page 115).

Felting
Vigorously washing crochet to shrink it and matt the fibres together (see page 64).

Filet
A type of crochet based on a regular mesh grid, with certain holes filled by extra stitches to form a pattern or a picture (see page 52).

Foundation chain
See Base chain.

French knot
An embroidery stitch (see page 59).

Front (of work)
The side of the work facing you as you work the current row or round.

Hexagon
A six-sided block (see page 121).

Hook, crochet hook
The tool used for most crochet work: a slim shaft of metal, wood or plastic with a hook at one end, available in many sizes (see page 8).

Intarsia
Another name for Picture crochet (see pages 60–63).

Lace (stitch pattern)
A stitch pattern forming an openwork design.

Ladder stitch
A sewn stitch used for assembly (see page 19).

Linen
Yarn spun from the fibres of flax plants.

Lurex
A metallic-effect yarn, normally spun from polyester and viscose.

Mercerized yarn
Yarn treated with chemicals to improve strength, lustre and reception to dye.

Mesh
A stitch pattern forming a regular geometric grid.

Natural fibre
Any yarn derived from animal products (such as wool) or vegetable products (such as cotton or linen).

Overcast seam
A sewn seam used for assembly (see page 19).

Picot
A loop of chain stitches, worked as part of a pattern, often along an edge (see page 116).

Picture crochet
A method of working pictorial designs from charts (see pages 60–63).

Puff (stitch)
Several stitches worked in the same place, and joined at the top (see page 115).

Raised (stitches)
Stitches formed by inserting the hook around the stem of a stitch below the normal position (see page 114).

Right side (of work)
The side that will be the outside of the finished piece.

Scallop
Another name for a shell or fan formation.

Shank
The small stem on the wrong side of some buttons, or a similar stem made with thread when attaching flat buttons.

Shell (stitch)
See Fan.

Silk
Yarn or thread spun from the cocoons of silkworms.

Slip knot
A simple knot used to begin crochet (see page 107).

Slip stitch
A crochet stitch (see page 108), or a sewn stitch used for assembly (see pages 19–20).

Spike
A stitch worked by inserting the hook from front to back, one or more rows below the normal position, and/or to the right or left (see page 117).

Stabiliser
Lightweight non-woven fabric, used to work embroidery (see pages 58–59).

Stitch marker
A small plastic device used to mark a particular stitch or row (see page 9).

Surface crochet
Decoration made by crocheting onto the surface of a piece of crochet (see page 55).

Synthetic (yarn)
Yarn spun from fibres derived from coal and petroleum products, to resemble natural fibre yarns (see page 11).

Tapestry needle
See Yarn needle.

Tension
The number of stitches and rows to a given measurement (see page 6).

Trim
A decorative length of crochet worked separately and sewn to a main piece.

Viscose
Yarn spun from a man-made fibre manufactured from cellulose.

Wool
Yarn spun from sheep's fleece.

Woven crochet
Contrasting yarns woven through the holes of a crochet mesh grid (see page 58).

Wrong side (of work)
The side that will be the inside of the finished piece.

Yarn needle
A blunt-tipped needle with a large eye (see page 9).

Index

Acknowledgements

With many thanks to Brown Sheep Company, Inc. who kindly supplied most of the yarns used in this book.

Quarto would also like to thank Shutterstock, for supplying images for inclusion in this book: p.9tr, p.9bl, p.11t.